PLAY LIKE A

PRO

72 PIANO ARRANGEMENTS
WITH THE PROFESSIONAL TOUCH

EDITED BY
STUART ISACOFF
AND
BECCA PULLIAM

Design by
Susanna Schavoir Koczeniak

Table of Contents

Taking It All In Stride

By Judy Carmichael

Fats Waller

Stride pianist Judy Carmichaels's recent appearance on CBS Sunday Morning with Charles Kurault caused a flood of phone calls to our offices inquiring about her book, Judy Carmichael's Complete Book Of Stride Piano *(published by Ekay Music). Judy is at work on some articles for us, and they will appear in the near future. Meanwhile, here's an excerpt from her book to help get those interested in the stride style on their way toward mastering this early jazz approach to the keyboard.*

Most early jazz piano was played in a stride style: a style featuring a bass pattern of single bass notes, octaves or tenths on the first and third beats and chords on the second and fourth. This sound, made famous by such legendary figures as James P. Johnson and Fats Waller, is staging a comeback, as more and more young musicians discover how joyous and dazzling this music can be.

Even if you don't want to specialize in this music, understanding the approach and attitude of the early stride players can add life and fun to all creative playing. Playing stride helps you to think, play and listen independently and to use your left-hand as a true rhythmic and harmonic compliment to your right-hand.

The exercises on the following pages are made up of standard figures, riffs and phrases associated with stride piano. They will build your "stride technique," and they can be utilized in a variety of ways.

Practice them until you can play the figures smoothly and in a "swinging" rhythm. Keep the time correct, but don't play too classically. Picture your fingers dancing over the keys; that's the feeling you want. You'll probably need to practice the left-hand separately, so you can make the jumps easily and not lose your time searching for bass notes.

Be sure you are able to play these figures well before you go on to performing full arrangements of stride pieces. This way you'll sight-read the actual music more easily, and you'll better hear how each device contributes to the melodic whole of a piece.

Remember to listen! Once you become comfortable with the approach, you can use snatches of the material for ornamentation and improvisation. Of course, none of these devices needs to be played exactly as written. Be creative. You can use only a part of a figure if you wish, or combine many figures.

Certain musical ideas will appeal to your ear more than others. Don't be afraid to use just those ideas that feel right to you. The ideas that stand out to *your* ears are original choices that only you can make. These choices will form the basis of your style. Trust your instincts, be creative, and have fun! ■

Judy Carmichael's Exercises For Stride Playing

7

AIN'T MISBEHAVIN'

Arranged by JUDY CARMICHAEL

HARRY BROOKS
ANDY RAZAF
THOMAS WALLER

10

"Ain't Misbehavin'"
A James P. Johnson Version

TRANSCRIBED BY RICCARDO SCIVALES

In April and June of 1944, shortly after the untimely death of Fats Waller, James P. Johnson recorded eight of Waller's famous hits, like *Ain't Misbehavin'*, *Squeeze Me, Honeysuckle Rose, My Fate Is In Your Hands,* etc. This was an affectionate tribute to his pupil and lifelong friend. Each song was recorded in two versions — as a piano solo (reissued on Swaggie S1211) and with the drum accompaniment of Eddie Dougherty (reissued on the CD *Snowy Morning Blues,* MCA GRP 16042).

This transcription of the second chorus of *Ain't Misbehavin'* — recorded on April 12, 1944 without drum accompaniment — shows us a facet of Johnson's later style, which sometimes was more linear and "economical" when compared with the thick and very complex textures he favored during the 20's and the 30's. Bars 1-5, 17-20, and 25-28 are a good example of that. As you can see, the melody is often single-noted, and in the accompaniment there are no "back beats" and almost no tenths. Nevertheless, in bars 7-8 James P. just can't resist the urge to spread his distinctive right hand tenth triads, and in other passages he gives some demonstrations of playing in double notes.

Perhaps this "simple" chorus of *Ain't Misbehavin'* cannot be counted among Johnson's recorded masterworks, but we hope you'll enjoy it all the same. After all, it is a delightful example of the stride style played by its master. Needless to say, the comparison between the Swaggie and the MCA GRP versions of *Ain't Misbehavin'* is very instructive about Johnson's outstanding improvisational skills. ■

Riccardo Scivales is the author of "Harlem Stride Piano Solos," published by Ekay Music.

13

ALFIE

Arranged by PRESTON KEYS

BURT BACHARACH & HAL DAVID

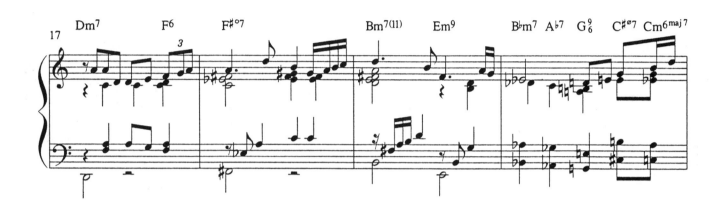
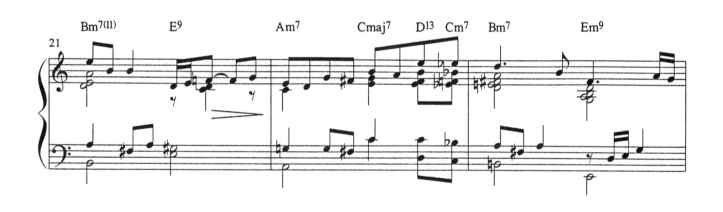

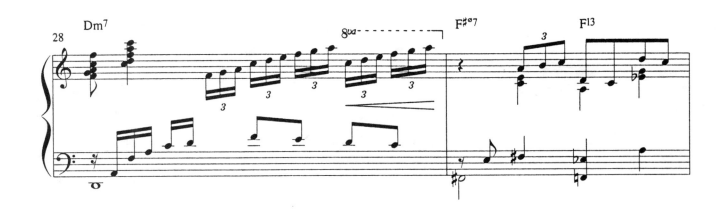

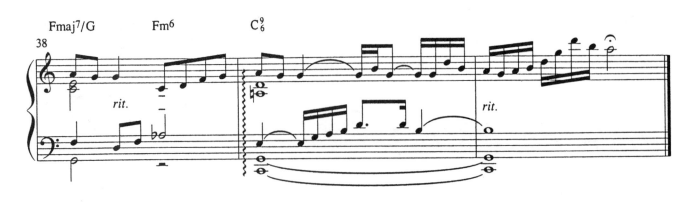

16

ANTIGUA

Arranged by CLAUS OGERMAN

ANTONIO CARLOS JOBIM
(1927-   )

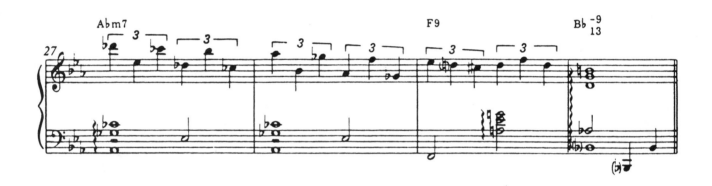

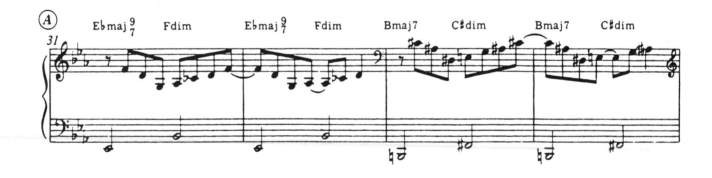

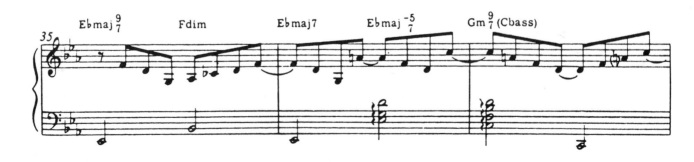

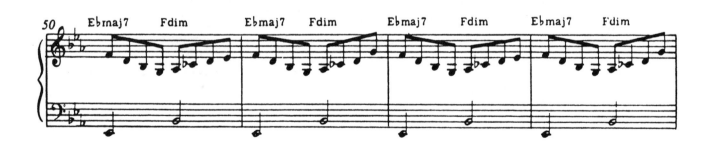

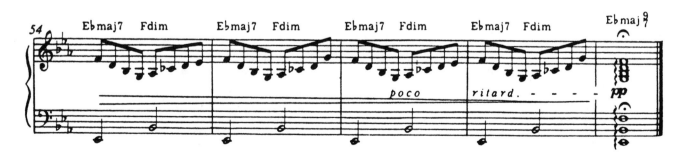

We love this elegant treatment with a touch of Gershwin by Phil Della Penna. Using the middle of a tune in the introduction, as suggested in the article following this piece of music, has worked very well in this arrangement.

BLUE MOON

Arranged by PHIL DELLA PENNA

LORENZ HART
RICHARD ROGERS

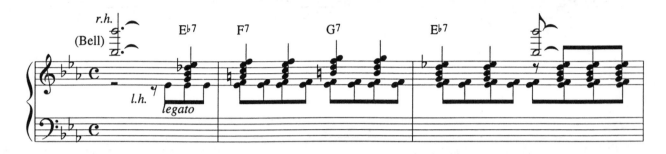

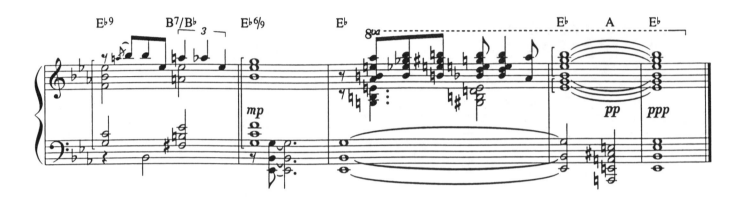

Introductions Are In Order

By David Leonhardt

The search for the perfect introduction seems like a never-ending task. Every song needs an intro of some kind, and each introduction should be unique to a particular song. A useful approach in creating an individual lead-in is to use the bridge of a song as the source of raw material for your introduction. The advantages of this are: 1) it suggests the song without "giving away" the identity; 2) it gives you a chance to play the bridge in case you have difficulty recalling it; and 3) it keeps all of your intros from sounding alike.

The bridge is commonly played "Ad Lib," with the actual tempo beginning at the end of the intro section or at the beginning of the song proper. I often play the bridge in another key, or use a few different keys to add interest, and to keep me awake (those of you who have done a four hour solo gig know that this is one of the biggest challenges a professional pianist faces).

Appearing on the following page is an example of an introduction for "Blue Moon," using the bridge as source material. Notice the first chord is a B Flat 7 flat nine with the right hand playing a G triad arpeggio. This chord-over-chord approach is a good way to find interesting-sounding arpeggios. Normally a dominant flat nine leads to the tonic but here I stay with the dominant for the beginning of the bridge and suspend the resolution until the end of the second bar.

Illustration by Art Glazer

In the third and fourth bars I reharmonize the melody for harmonic interest, which leads us to the textural change in the fifth measure. Here I put some left hand scalar runs in: first the A Flat Dorian Minor scale, then the D Flat Diminished scale, and finally the A Flat pentatonic scale in both hands over the G Flat Major chord. I end the intro with a series of chromatic minor seventh chords to bring us back to the B Flat dominant chord. This resolves nicely to the first chord of the song — an E Flat Major.

Try using the bridges of other songs for your own introductions. Keep in mind that the fundamental purposes of a good intro are to state the mood or the feel of the song, to establish the key, and to set the tempo of the piece. Rely on your ear to tell you if it works or not, and please let me know if it helps you stay awake on your next solo gig!

A Sample Introduction
To "Blue Moon"

BUT BEAUTIFUL

Arranged by MARK LEVINE

Words by JOHNNY BURKE
Music by JIMMY VAN HEUSEN

CELIA

Transcribed by BECCA PULLIAM

EARL (BUD) POWELL
(1924-1966)

An arrangement of "Celia" and Bud Powell''s solo on it, as well as five other Powell compositions, are published in Jazz Masters: Bud Powell by
Clifford Jay Safane, available from Music Sales Corporation, 24 East 22nd St., New York, NY 10010. Catalog number 040082.

etc.

CEORA

Arranged by NOREEN SAULS

LEE MORGAN
(1938-1972)

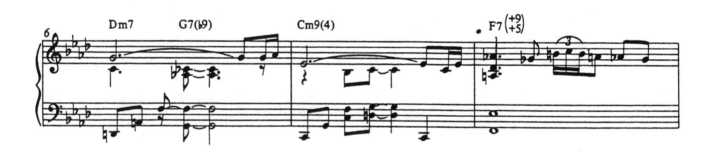

* *Trill on this note in original recording.*

29

A

‖: AbMa7 ∕ ∕ ∕ | Bbm7 ∕ Eb7 ∕ | AbMa7 ∕ ∕ ∕ | Ebm7 ∕ Ab7 ∕ |

DbMa7 ∕ ∕ ∕ | Dm7 ∕ G7 ∕ | Cm7 ∕ ∕ ∕ | F7 ∕ ∕ ∕ |

Bbm7 ∕ ∕ ∕ | Eb7 ∕ ∕ ∕ | Cm7 ∕ ∕ ∕ | F7 ∕ ∕ ∕ |

Dm7 ∕ ∕ ∕ | G7 ∕ ∕ ∕ | Cm7 ∕ F7 ∕ | Bbm7 ∕ Eb7 ∕ ‖

B

‖ AbMa7 ∕ ∕ ∕ | Bbm7 ∕ Eb7 ∕ | AbMa7 ∕ ∕ ∕ | Ebm7 ∕ D7(+5) ∕ |

DbMa7 ∕ ∕ ∕ | Dm7 ∕ G7 ∕ | Cm7 ∕ ∕ ∕ | F7 ∕ ∕ ∕ |

Bbm7 ∕ ∕ ∕ | Eb7 ∕ ∕ ∕ | Cm7(b5) ∕ ∕ ∕ | F7 ∕ ∕ ∕ |

Bbm7 ∕ ∕ ∕ | Eb7 sus4 ∕ ∕ ∕ | AbMa7 ∕ ∕ ∕ | Bbm7 ∕ Eb7 ∕ :‖

Some notes about "Ceora"

The trumpeter Lee Morgan recorded this lovely tune on *Cornbread* (Blue Note CD7 842222). Noreen Sauls plays it on the recent album *Ceora* under the leadership of reed player James L. Dean (Cexton CR 8158). From a bossa nova introduction, a poised and fluid melody emerges, and I think this melody is better every time I play it.

I took the arrangement to Linda Ferri, an accomplished classical pianist with an ability that I admire to make music come from the printed page. Linda points out how the first three phrases of the melody sound like a comment on a comment on a comment. The phrases descend. As they come down, you can play each a little less loudly. In the sixth measure following **A**, Noreen has answered them with an ascending left hand figure that deserves to be heard. At **B**, when the melody rises, the music builds. But don't ignore the opportunities for dynamics within each phrase — the big picture contains some smaller designs.

I also find, as I've learned to sing "Ceora,"

that I've improved my recognition of the descending diminished scale. The pick-ups to the F at bar 9 are a descending half step-whole step scale. The pick-ups to measure 11 are the same scale, transposed down a half-step. The pick-ups to measure 17 are a diminished scale leading to C.

Noreen draws your attention to the left hand rhythm at measure 17. "The pattern of E♮s results in an interesting cross-rhythm and syncopation. It's like duple against triple meter. Maybe a simple exercise could come out of this." You can devise one by playing the left hand over and over, and improvising in 4/4 with the right.

We include a chart of the song (above) so you can improvise your own choruses before returning to Noreen's arrangement for the vamp and final chord. It includes a tritone interval (three whole steps).

— Becca Pulliam

30

A Pianistic Tribute To Stan Getz

By Andy LaVerne

When I was a young child, my parents would spend the summer with the family in Chappaqua, a quiet, picturesque village just 20 miles north of the hustle and bustle of New York City. Years later, as a member of the Stan Getz quartet, I wrote a ballad for Stan. In my search for a title, I remembered those tranquil summers with the family in Chappaqua, and I knew that I had found the title I was searching for. Stan Getz's lyricism set him apart from all other players, and it was this characteristic that served as the seed for the melodic development of *Chappaqua*.

Stan's improvisations were always deep within the harmonies, and it was his penchant for diatonic playing that helped shape the harmonic aspect of the tune. If asked to play a "medley of my hit," it would most certainly be *Chappaqua*. It became a staple of Stan's group, and we played it virtually every night for almost three years.

Even after I left the group, Stan continued to play it. We recorded it on the album "Live At Midem" (RCA). I also recorded it with John Abercrombie on a project produced by Stan but never released.

Chappaqua got some more play in my three year tenure with Chris and Dan Brubeck in our group BLT (Brubeck/LaVerne Trio). Just three years ago I recorded it again, this time with Chuck Loeb on the album "Magic Fingers" (DMP). Chuck and I were on Stan's band together for a couple of years. And last year, pianist Richie Beirach (another Getz band alumnus), using the Yamaha Disclavier, recorded a fantastic extrapolation of *Chappaqua* on the soon-to-be-released CD, "Universal Mind" (Steeplechase).

Finally, though, I gave *Chappaqua* a rest from my repertoire, until a few months ago when I did my "Live at Maybeck Hall" recording for Concord Jazz. This seemed an ideal opportunity to dedicate the piece to Stan on a recording, especially since it was Stan who introduced me to Carl Jefferson (owner of Concord Jazz) some years ago.

I learned a lot while playing with Stan. Melodic development heads the list. Getz's ability to take a simple melodic cell, and over the course of a solo develop it by means of melodic embellishment, sequence, modulation, and rhythmic variation made him a master of melodic invention. Notice how the first melodic statement in *Chappaqua* is echoed in the subsequent phrases,

using the devices mentioned above. The use of the interval of a sixth (major & minor) interspersed with diatonic scalar passages lends a lyrical and diatonic quality to the melody, not unlike Stan's approach to melodic improvisation. The use of incremental half steps in the melody and harmony from measures 19-25 is another technique favored by Getz.

Perhaps the most important lesson imparted to me by Stan was in regard to projection of sound. When I first started with Stan, he mentioned that I was not projecting enough to the audience. It took me a while to understand what he meant. He was not talking about the volume or loudness of the tone I produced from the piano, but rather the fullness of the tone, regardless of the volume. In performance, a pianist must be able to get a full, round tone from the instrument, so that the music projects to the audience no matter what dynamic is being played. By playing *Chappaqua* with Stan so much, I was given the opportunity to develop the ability to project while playing pianissimo. This gave me control to use tone production in louder tunes as well.

The key to this is in using the weight from the back and shoulders, and transferring it through the arms, wrists, and fingers. The mistake I was making initially was playing mainly from the arms and fingers. When I discovered the answer to Stan's request for projection, and actually delivered on the gig, Stan's look of recognition told me I had reached a new plateau in my playing.

In the Maybeck version of *Chappaqua*, which is solo piano, I use another technique I have been developing since my days with Stan, reharmonization. I think Stan would have enjoyed playing on my new set of changes almost as much as he enjoyed the original changes. I close the Maybeck performance with a final reading of the melody with the original changes, as presented here. I imagined that Stan was playing the melody with me, as he had countless times, and the tone emanating from the piano was fuller than it had ever been. A tranquil feeling came over me, much as it had when I was spending a summer in Chappaqua. ∎

CHAPPAQUA

ANDY LaVERNE

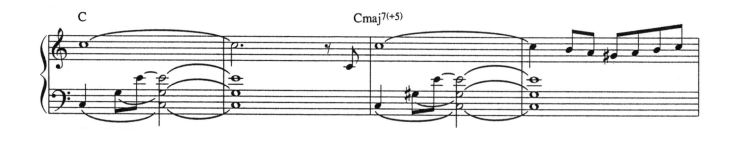

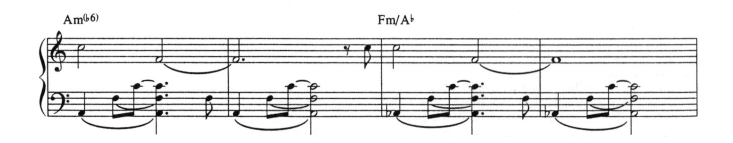

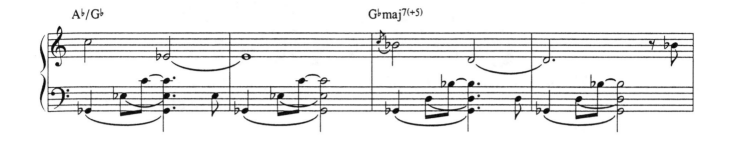

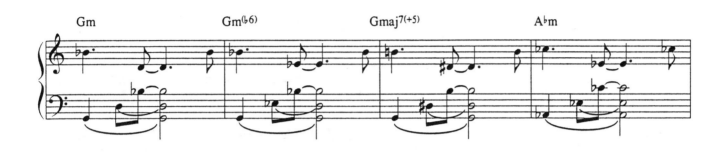

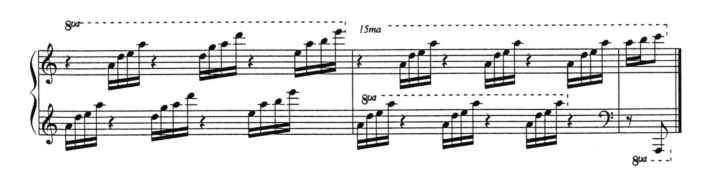

33

CHATTANOOGA CHOO CHOO

as arranged by Riccardo Scivales, author of Harlem Stride Piano Solos, *in typical boogie style*

Music by HARRY WARREN

An offbeat etude

Brazilian rhythmic figures articulate the offbeats—the "ands" of the beats. Playing an entire accompaniment in this fashion is excellent for stabilizing your rhythm and feeling the offbeats. Take a beautiful, singing melody, such as Jobim's "Chega de Saudade" ("No More Blues") and accompany it with an offbeat pattern. Anticipate the chord changes by a half beat. You must know where beat one is even though you don't play on it. The result — if you move the voices in the left hand as little as possible in making the change — is ever so subtle.

There are ways to relieve the monotony of an exercise like this.

Sing the melody as you play It with your right hand. Vary the melody and sing along. Voice the melody, with full voicings or just an occasional, melancholy second thickening a note.

Thicken the chords in the left hand. Play some alternative chord changes. In the case of "Chega de Saudade," the harmonic rhythm (frequency of chord changes) moves slowly enough so that you can insert a neighboring or passing chord occasionally. Or make substitutions. And finally, start to relieve the unbroken procession of offbeats with new rhythmic figures in the left hand — figures that retain the offbeat feeling yet offer variety.

CHEGA DE SAUDADE

Arranged by BECCA PULLIAM

A. C. JOBIM
(1927-   )

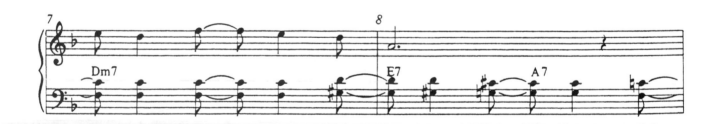

Original text by Vinticus De Moreas. Music by Antonio Carlos Jobim. © 1962, 1967 Editora Musical Aarpua, Soa Paulo, Brazil.
TRO-Hollis Music Inc., New York, controls all rights for the USA and Canada. Used by Permission.

Song continues with a B section.

Dick Hyman's version of this Ellington gem can be heard on his new recording, "Dick Hyman Plays Duke Ellington" (Reference Recordings RR50 DCD).

—THE CLOTHED WOMAN—

Arranged by DICK HYMAN

DUKE ELLINGTON

* Right hand only *sfz* and louder than left, simile throughout.

39

40

41

Jazz Harmony: *"Danny Boy"*

By Noreen Sauls

A solo piano arrangement contains many different elements that bear consideration: chord voicings, progressions, various textures, the way a melody moves, bass lines, and so on. In this article, we'll examine some of these as they occur in my arrangement of "Danny Boy," beginning on the next page. Once you have studied the devices used, and understand their functions, you will be able to apply them to other tunes.

First, let's look at **chord movement**. Besides the more common ii-V (which you'll find in measures 4 and 9 of section A), there are those based on chromatic movement of the bass line (see measures 11-15 of A).

Various chord types are constructed underneath the melody. **Whole step motion** is present in the introduction and in the third and fourth measures from the end of the piece. Each chord in the sequence is a whole step lower than the previous one, so the TYPE of chord does not change.

Tritone motion (a tritone is described by the interval of an augmented fourth) occurs in measures 6 and 7 of A. Look at the bass line:

In between each tritone there is chromatic movement.

Voicings are always a "hot topic" among pianists. Who isn't always searching for new ones to add to the "repertoire"? First consider texture ... thick or thin? The answer depends on the effect you want. Chords can have just a few notes in them (as in measures 1 and 2, or 12-15 of section B)…

or they can have many (as in measure 4 of B, beats 2, 3 and 4).

Using both is a nice way to provide contrast. Big, wide, open harmonies sound great, but chances are, some things will not be easily reachable for smaller hands, as in the left hand part of measures 8-10 in section B. In that case, the chord must be rolled from bottom to top, catching the lowest note in the pedal and using the middle note as a midpoint of balance for your hand. Take any of the examples cited here and practice rolling up and down the keyboard. (While you're at it, give the right hand a workout too. This way, you'll be prepared for anything.)

Sometimes, a note from the left hand can be taken comfortably in the right hand (as in measure 7 of A), eliminating the need to roll, so check out that possibility as well. Whatever you decide, remember in voicing chords to leave more space in between the notes as you move into the lower register. Intervals such as fifths, sevenths, tenths and octaves can prevent muddiness in the left hand.

Voicings can be rootless, as in measure 10 of A, beats 2, 3 and 4. Or they can appear with roots firmly on the bottom, as in measure 4 of B.

Harmonic movement (the number of chords per measure) can be slow (as in measures 1 and 15 of A and measures 9 and 15 of B),

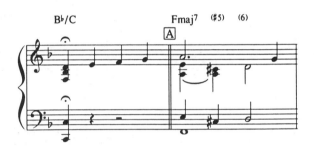

or fast (as in measures 6, 8 and 10 of A and measure 4 of B). Again, a balance is good for contrast. (Two chords per measure is about average.)

As you play the piece, you will notice that some voicings have **doubled notes**, and some do not. Why? I make the decision not based on any rules, but by sound. The doubled tones can provide strength, emphasis and enhancement, or it can overpower and create imbalance. Each situation is different. Experiment — your ears will be the best guide. In measure 1 of A, we have doubling of the inner voices. Here it provides movement as well. Sometimes I like to think of choral or instrumental groups when playing or writing. Other examples of inner voice writing may be found in measures 1, 5, 9, 11 and 12 of section B. Notice the harmonic and rhythmic interest they add.

Observe the **slash chords** used in the notation. Some are polychords (as in measure 7 of A — Am7/G7), and can be called by another name (G11 in this case). Others identify bass movement (as in measure 3 of section B on beat 4). Finally, some simply indicate an inversion of a chord (as in measure 11 of B, beat 1 and measure 13 of B, beat 1).

As you play through the arrangement, see what other elements and examples you can find, to add to your musical vocabulary. Then, try writing you own arrangement of a favorite tune! ■

DANNY BOY

Arranged by NOREEN SAULS

TRADITIONAL

Marian McPartland's Piano Jazz

The radio program begins with a short theme by piano and bass.

Then the announcer says,

"From New York, this is **Marian McPartland's Piano Jazz,** *a colorful kaleidoscope of great keyboard artists from the world of jazz, hosted by talented composer/pianist Marian McPartland." Marian McPartland's on the air.*

There isn't a reader who wouldn't trade places with Marian McPartland. For seven years she's been host and co-conspirator at the keyboard for her own weekly program on National Public Radio. She's featured over one hundred pianists, each in an hour of conversation and music — solos and two-piano duets. At least once a show, Marian plays a solo of her own, usually a McPartland original.

The program brims with musical empathy and communication, including lots of shop talk. Challenged by McPartland on the subject of his formative years ("I don't think you had any formative years"), Oscar Peterson defended himself. Yes, as everyone else, he had had to learn the vocabulary of jazz. He'd tutored himself, singing a run as he taught his right hand to play it, then his left hand. He demonstrated the process, using a bluesy run something like this.

Since the advent of his solo period, he said, he has had to learn to play different lines simultaneously in each hand. For example,

Peterson made the fundamental observation that the two hands are different. The thumb's on the left side of one set of fingers, on the right side of the other! Fingerings for the same run are not identical. From this, said Oscar Peterson, flows everything you need to know about playing two-handed piano.

Bill Evans and Marian McPartland stepped into the thick of four-handed two-piano duets immediately. Evans tried to describe the improvisational technique of rhythmically displacing a phrase, and McPartland said "Show me." So, on Cole Porter's "All of You," with McPartland keeping time and playing a Bb pedal tone, Evans recycled a complicated three-beat

phrase. A sketch of the result would look something like this.

After the duet, an exhilarated Marian exclaimed, "That felt like swimming against the tide!"

Detroit delicate

Barry Harris opened his program with a faithful performance of Bud Powell's recording of "I'll Keep Loving You," beginning with the lovely introduction (see boxed example).

"Bud's records were my school," said Harris, as he casually played some additional Powell signatures, such as the ending to "Parisian Thoroughfare."

Harris deprecated his own touch, calling it "Detroit delicate," and confided that he would prefer to have a heavier, more aggressive "East Coast" touch, like Thelonious Monk's. Then he talked about some of his teaching experiences, and played one of the pieces he assigns his students, the TV theme from the original "I Love Lucy" series.

Roger Kellaway and McPartland played two pianos on one of Kellaway's compositions — the slightly honky-tonk TV theme from "All in the Family." Afterwards, they laughed about throwing elbows, and Kellaway quoted the composer Edgar Varèse regarding the "distance from forearm to elbow as a splash of percussive color

on the keyboard." McPartland noticed that Kellaway had inserted a scalewise improvisation on the John Coltrane "Giant Steps" chord progression on Kellaway's improvisation on "I'm Getting Sentimental Over You."

That led to a brief discussion of Nicolas Slonimsky's **Thesaurus of Scales** which Kellaway called "Coltrane's Bible, at least for awhile."

Ellis Marsalis played his composition "Syndrome," developed on the job. In his case, the job was teaching at the New Orleans Center for the Creative Arts. His students included his sons, Wynton and Branford, and other young talents on the national scene today, such as Terence Blanchard and Donald Harrison, Jr. "I created little chord progressions on the spot for the kids," said Marsalis, "like problems to be solved." The solution required was to fit an original melody with the chord progression. "Syndrome's" opening root movement resembles "Giant Steps" — D to G to Bb — but then it goes back to D. And the chord qualities are all major. In the end, "pieces write themselves anyway," Marsalis commented.

Mother-style piano

When Dick Hyman came on the program, McPartland asked him about his musical background. He said he'd been a "jazz nut" from very early, that his big brother had been his musical inspiration, but that he'd also taken some encouragement from his mother. "My mother played with a lot of loud pedal like mothers do. Why do they do that?" he asked rhetorically, as he demonstrated "mother-style" at his keyboard. From her keyboard, McPartland responded in her mother's style, with a snippet of Chopin.

no pedal (or not much)

Later in the program, Hyman and McPartland jointly improvised a very successful duet, which she called a "free thing" and Hyman described as having "no particular plan."

Kellaway had advised the pianists in the radio audience that free improvisation should constitute half their practice time, following the fifty percent devoted to building technique and learning the repertoire. On the subject of practicing, Bill Evans said, "It's better to play one tune for 24 hours than 24 tunes for one hour each." He also confessed that he had attended no more than four rehearsals in twenty years. Jimmy Rowles described a device which he had had made for his piano — a mute that muffled the sound — so that he could come home after a night on the job and continue to play into the wee hours of the morning. That's when he truly mastered stride piano, he said, starting very slowly and gradually increasing the size of the leaps.

Rowles talked about the influences of Carl Perkins and Ellis Larkins, and turned a nice phrase to describe accompanying a singer: "making a carpet."

Duke Ellington's name has come up again and again on **Marian McPartland's Piano Jazz**. Cedar Walton recalled Ellington's twice annual visits to Walton's hometown, Dallas. For him, Ellington was an "early model." Walton slyly quoted the melody from "Love You Madly" in his interpretation of "My Ship," and improvised on the figure from Randy Weston's "High Fly"

during "I Didn't Know What Time It Was." John Lewis said he made a point of never meeting Duke Ellington or Art Tatum because they were gods to him. And Bill Evans, when he played Ellington's "Reflections in D," noted that there was no need to improvise because the melody was so beautiful.

McPartland confines herself to no single era or style of jazz. One recent enjoyable program featured Kenny Kirkland. After several years with Wynton Marsalis's group, Kirkland was hired by the rock musician Sting. McPartland had boned up on even that, and she played one of the themes from the album **Dream of the Blue Turtles** to Kirkland.

They discussed the effect of electronic sequencers on some of the themes, for example this one, where the right hand figure is repeated over and over in the same key, and the left hand moves.

Kirkland's development in jazz was most greatly influenced by Herbie Hancock, Chick Corea and McCoy Tyner, he said, and he's now working back through the other giants. "I have to get grounded in Bud Powell." As one of his solos, he chose Thelonious Monk's recorded version of the classic "Just You, Just Me," and McPartland mentioned that Lester Young had also recorded the tune. The Kirkland / McPartland duets were extremely successful, suffering not the slightest from a generation gap.

McPartland's aware of the need to make a mix of guests, drawing from the well-known, the (in her words) "dyed-in-the-wool" artists who set the standards for the scene but whose names are not so well-known, and the women artists because there are "so many good women around." She recently invited Jane Jarvis on the show. Besides her career as a jazz pianist, Jarvis has had other careers — as organist at Shea Stadium (home of the Mets) in New York, and as producer for Muzak.

It's the shared language of jazz that makes McPartland's mix work, and her own talents as an interviewer, solo and duo pianist, and a repertoire of "thousands" of songs. "I've been doing shows for seven years now. It started out to be a series of 13. Now, I can't bear the thought of ever giving it up." Devoted listeners — many who listen for tips on how to play jazz piano — surely agree.●

—Becca Pulliam

A DELICATE BALANCE

MARIAN McPARTLAND

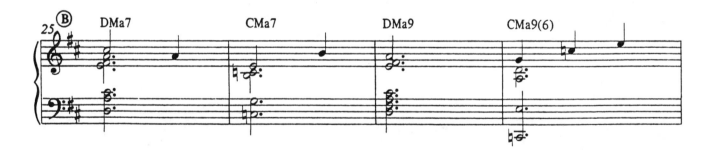

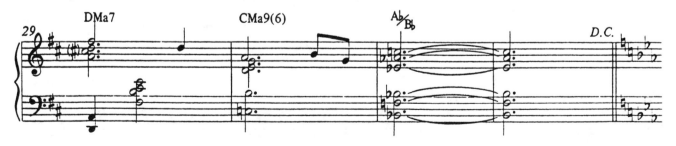

© Copyright 1972 by Halcyon Music. Used by Permission.

51

Three ways to play a glissando

When Phil Della Penna plays "Don't Blame Me," he chooses the notes and chords with the care of an orchestrator. Notice, for example, how he builds chords with three widely spaced notes in the left hand and triads in the right, the melody note doubled an octave lower. Della Penna encourages you, the reader, to thin out the chords if you wish, to match your taste or ability.

He reharmonizes and stylizes the standard with a movie director's sense of drama. The last A of the AABA form is a study in itself. Della Penna modulates from F to the key of Ab for eight measures, then to C for a reprise. You may want to analyze these key changes to see how they are accomplished, and listen carefully for the emotional effect. The climax comes six measures later, and Della Penna marks it with a dramatic pause.

The other device in "Don't Blame Me" is the glissando. Here's how Phil executes it: 1. In measure 15, he pulls the right thumbnail down the white keys. To double the thickness, he plays the gliss in thirds, dragging his third fingertip behind the thumbnail, two keys behind. 2. In measure 38, he plays the descending glissando two-handed. He drags the nails of the fingers (excluding thumb) of his left hand down the black notes. The back of the hand faces the keyboard. The right hand follows a half step or so behind, dragging the nails down the white keys. The right hand is curled under from the wrist. 3. In measures 42-43, he does the opposite. The right nails run up the black keys, the left up the white. The left hand is curled. Happy sledding! .

DON'T BLAME ME

Arranged by PHIL DELLA PENNA

DOROTHY FIELDS
JIMMY McHUGH

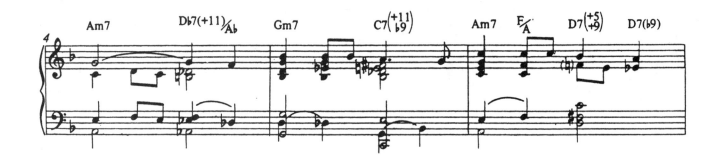

53

54

"Don't Blame Me" is from a Mary Lou Williams folio put out by Robbins Music in the 40's. It is not known whether the pianist wrote out her arrangement, recorded it for someone else to transcribe or allowed someone to write in her style. But her name was on the book. My recollection is that Mary Lou kept the tempo with her foot, and I suggest that you do the same as you play "Don't Blame Me" so that it doesn't sag. It is even more lovely in tempo than rubato.

Williams' 1945 Zodiac Suite was recently performed for the second time ever (first was in 1945) at Duke University, where she was teaching when she died.

—Becca Pulliam

DON'T BLAME ME

Arranged by MARY LOU WILLIAMS

DOROTHY FIELDS
JIMMY McHUGH

56

Dave Brubeck — It's About Time

BY STUART ISACOFF

"There's a myth that I'm a classical pianist," says Dave Brubeck with some consternation. The legendary pianist/composer, whose experiments with time and polytonality have assured him a unique place in jazz history, has often been, he insists, mislabeled, and he'd like to set the record straight. Some critics, noting his penchant for odd meters and thick, complex harmonies, and aware that he studied at one point with composer Darius Milhaud, have attributed to Brubeck a tendency toward the musically cool-blooded and rational— toward, in other words, certain elements of the European classical tradition. "I have never played a classical piece, beyond 'Hanging Gardens' and 'Barcarolle,'" he insists. "My early technical training was zero. My mother, who was my first piano teacher, gave up on me, and so did everybody else along the way. I had some good, well-trained teachers tell me to forget it."

From time to time he considered the possibility. Brubeck was raised on a ranch—he spent hours on horseback working out rhythmic figures to accompany the clippity-clop of hooves—and the thought crossed his mind more than once to return. But along with practical training in the ways of ranching, he was instilled early on with a love of music, and it has carried him through the rough times. "In our house you just heard piano music from the first thing in the morning 'till you fell asleep at night," he remembers, "because my mother taught most of the day and she practiced after dinner; she would practice for hours, and that was what I'd hear while I was falling asleep."

That music was not jazz. Yet Dave Brubeck knew exactly what he wanted to play from the moment he sampled what he describes as "the joy of Fats Waller." This too he discovered at home. One of his earliest musical memories is, he says, of "the joy I always felt when I heard my brother Amory rehearse his band at our house on Thursday nights; I was absolutely thrilled with jazz from the time I first heard it." Once he listened to the recordings of Albert Ammons, Teddy Wilson and Billy Kyle, the conversion was complete.

Those early influences are apparent, even on such modern musical outings as the fantastically popular recording *Time Out*, which features saxophonist Paul Desmond's 5/4 meter hit tune, "Take Five." He produces a sound deep into the keys, solidly anchored to the pulse of the music, and frequently hinting at Barrelhouse origins. But Brubeck has always been a musical free spirit: "Even as a kid," he relates, "I had trouble with my rhythm sections; I was always experimenting with time." By the time he was performing professionally, his rhythmic ideas had developed to the point of pushing fellow band members beyond their abilities. "One night I had a rhythm section that was telling me I was wrong," he remembers. "I went to drummer Shelly Manne and said, 'Shelly, I want you to listen to me tonight; watch my foot, because the guys say my foot is off and it's driving them crazy.' When I walked off stage he said, 'Your foot is like a metronome; the guys are off.'"

It wasn't until he formed his best-known quartet, featuring drummer Joe Morello, that those rhythmic ideas could come to full fruition. At the same time, the pianist and his group came in for some strong criticism for the direction they were taking. Miles Davis, for one, said they didn't swing, and the accusation has been echoed over the years.

One of the reasons for this may be in the way the pianist works with structure. A Brubeck solo has virtually nothing to do with running slick melodic patterns up and down the keyboard over a set of chord changes. His improvisational approach is, he admits, "like the way you would approach composition: take an idea and build on it." Sometimes the result resembles a progression of musical building blocks, rather than the more commonly-heard seamless stream of lines. What's more, there is no predicting where his improvisations might lead. "You know," says Dave Brubeck, "people who have taped me illegally night after night are amazed that they don't know what's going to happen in a given tune. I don't know what's going to happen. I always try to make it different, even if it's going to turn out badly; I take chances and don't work things out."

Another clue might lie in his manipulation of metrical accents. Where a player like McCoy Tyner will often shift, within a 4/4 meter piece, into accent groups of 3 —"heating up" the energy level—Dave Brubeck might take a piece in 3/4 time—as he does in "Kathy's Waltz"—and reorganize the pulse into a more leisurely grouping of 4, thus "cooling" things down. Nevertheless, his music's popularity is proof enough that there is plenty of swing behind it.

Brubeck's harmonies can be dense and colorful, but here, too, there is a purposefulness behind each sound —an approach that is "classical" in the best sense. Darius Milhaud once told him that the problem with twelve-tone music is that you don't get a sense of where you're going. Some would say that jazz went through a period some years ago in which everything became similarly aimless. "One of my favorite pianists," he relates, "told me that one of his students said, 'I don't want to play any chords with roots, because it's not exciting; it doesn't sound good.' This guy said, 'Yeah? Well, listen to Brubeck; there's always a root.' There's not always a root, but I'm always *thinking* of the root; that's for sure." The result can still be adventurous. C~ne of Brubeck's best-known tunes, "The Duke," was originally entitled "The Duke Meets Darius Milhaud," in tribute to two of his most important influences, and it travels all over the map tonally. Miles Davis recorded "The Duke," and another Brubeck favorite, "In Your Own Sweet Way," which is also known for its strange musical twists. In fact, it's been the center of some controversy. "Have you seen John Mehegan's analysis of 'In Your Own Sweet Way'?" Brubeck asks. "He swears the tune is in B Flat, and that's how it appears in most fakebooks. I wrote it in E Flat, and I would argue the point with him, but I couldn't win. Then Miles insisted on playing that E natural in the eighth bar of the tune. I asked him why and he said that's the way I wrote it." That's another technical point that has remained unresolved. Now, both versions have been recorded by dozens of artists.

And what is he up to these days? In addition to a heavy performing and touring schedule, Dave Brubeck has devoted a great deal of time in recent years to writing sacred music and pieces for large ensembles. New recordings are being released on the MusicMasters label, and Columbia Legacy has just issued a boxed set called "Time Signatures—A Career Retrospective." It's a 4-CD package that demonstrates the enormous breadth of his work over the years, in collaboration with such artists as Cal Tjader, Paul Desmond, Leonard Bernstein, Louis Armstrong, Charles Mingus, Gerry Mulligan and others. The classical group *An die Musik* has commissioned his latest work: an original piece based on Bach's *Chromatic Fantasy And Fuglle,* to be premiered in March at the Kennedy Center and in Germany. But jazz musicians who acknowledge they have been influenced by him—from Cecil Taylor, who has said that Dave Brubeck filled an important gap in the jazz piano lineage, to Denny Zeitlin, Bill Evans, Chick Corea, Jessica Williams and others—will always consider him one of their own.

Andy LaVerne has performed extensively with members of the Brubeck family.
This is his arrangement of one of his favorite Brubeck hits.

THE DUKE

Arranged by ANDY LaVERNE

DAVE BRUBECK

Ecuadorean Memories

BY BUTCH THOMPSON

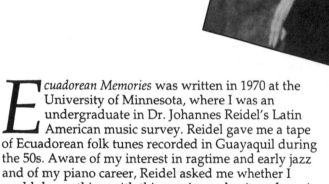

E cuadorean Memories was written in 1970 at the University of Minnesota, where I was an undergraduate in Dr. Johannes Reidel's Latin American music survey. Reidel gave me a tape of Ecuadorean folk tunes recorded in Guayaquil during the 50s. Aware of my interest in ragtime and early jazz and of my piano career, Reidel asked me whether I could do anything with this music — play it, reshape it, whatever. The result was several new pieces based on the Ecuadorean originals. I later traveled to Ecuador to find out more about the music, but this piece, I confess, was written and titled before I had ever seen the place.

In typical ragtime fashion, there are four distinct themes, embellished by an intro and interlude which are both based on the third theme in C minor. The intro is followed by a 32-bar section which incorporates two 16-bar themes. The first is my own invention, based on the ragtime convention of three-against-two; the second is an authentic Ecuadorean two-step (*sanjuanito*) just slightly altered by syncopation.

After the repeat and the interlude, the third 32-bar section — another authentic folk melody — is played twice, the second time in octaves and with some syncopated decorations. The final section is another invention of mine which, like the opening section, combines ragtime syncopation with South American melancholy. This bittersweet quality comes from the nebulous major-minor tonality of all four themes. The folk tune beginning at the 17th bar of the first section is a beautiful example of this: when the melody is played without its harmonic underpinnings, it sounds like a pleasant ditty in C major, even resolving on a C; the last

two bars of the harmonic structure, however, take us out of the major tonality and into the relative A minor via an inexorable E7 in bar 30. All four sections of the piece use this strategy.

The piece should be played as a brisk two-step; this is in the manner of early ragtime, based on vigorous dance music.

A pianist who specializes in ragtime and early jazz turns to South America for inspiration.

Known to millions for his work on public radio's "A Prairie Home Companion," pianist Butch Thompson has for much longer been internationally recognized as a leading performer of vintage jazz and ragtime. "Ecuadorean Memories" has been issued on the solo piano recording "New Orleans Joys," Daring CD 3001 and cassette C 3001.

─ECUADOREAN MEMORIES─

Music by BUTCH THOMPSON

65

EVERYTHING HAPPENS TO ME

Arranged by MATT DENNIS

TOM ADAIR & MATT DENNIS

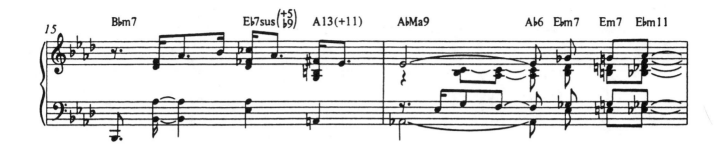

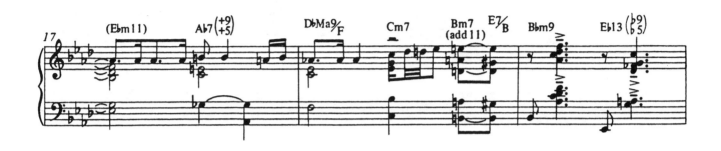

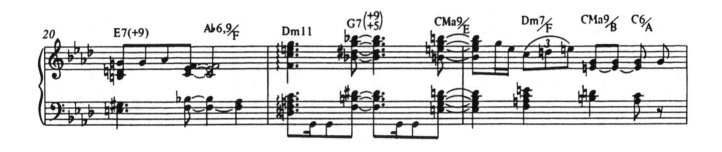

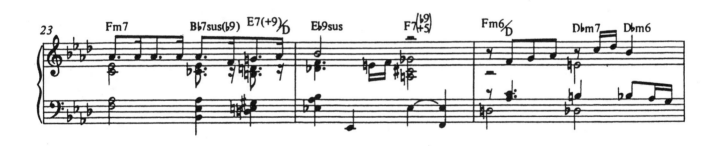

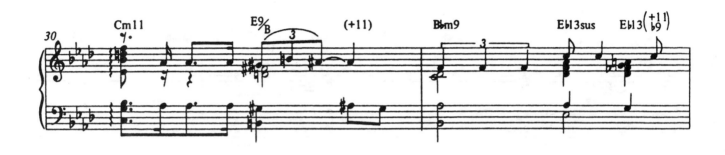

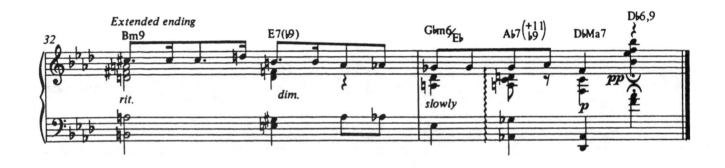

Jazz Harmony: The Gershwin Connection

BY STUART ISACOFF

The sophisticated harmonies of modern jazz piano—especially the tight, clustered left-hand voicings and "extended" or upper-partial right hand chords that achieved such prominence through the playing of the late and ever popular Bill Evans—are usually attributed to the influence of turn-of-the-century French Impressionists such as Debussy and Ravel. This is especially true of cases such as this stream of chromatically shifting augmented ninth and thirteenth chords, in Ravel's *Gaspard de la nuit:*

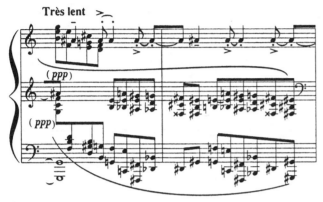

or in the coiled but ambiguous harmonies of Russia's (and Paris's) Alexander Scriabin, originator of the so called "mystical chord":

Such dominant harmonies, moving in half-step shifts ~cross the keyboard, permeate jazz—in forms like the ravel example above, and in similarly colorful jazz voicings like these:

There is no denying the European connection. Yet, it an American music legend—George Gershwin— who deserves much of the credit for synthesizing and shaping the elements of what has now become standard jazz harmony. Most jazz performers concede a debt of gratitude to this composer for providing them with the chord changes of "I Got Rhythm." Those changes are a fairly ubiquitous presence today as a framework for improvised solos. Sadly, though, Gershwin's personal style—a hybrid of honky-tonk, Impressionism, early jazz, blues and more (he even dabbled in Viennese expressionist techniques toward the end of his life)— is given little credit for having had an impact on contemporary performance.

Gershwin deserves much of the credit for shaping modern jazz harmony.

George Gershwin was clearly influenced by the French Impressionists, but his contribution to the art of playing and composing went far beyond their sound world, into something distinctly American. When Ravel used "jazz" chords, for example, it was with a broad rush, to create a wash of color. Gershwin used them Functionally, in support of a melody, and with careful consideration of how they worked within a framework of the musical tension and relaxation. Gershwin was preoccupied with good melody and counter-melody, which brought a focused directness to his writing. And his rhythmic approach was a swinging refutation of Ravel's fuzzy lilt.

An interesting example of Gershwin's work — one that has survived as a harmonic example for later generations — can be found in his setting of "My Man's Gone Now," from the opera Porgy And Bess.

Note the shifting three-note chords over a D pedal point in the following excerpt:

The pungent chords used in measures 3 and 4—in a chromatic sequence representing I-V (D7+9 moving to an A13)—are familiar to anyone playing jazz, pop or even rock. They are built in combinations of perfect and augmented fourths rather than in thirds; and they are surrounded in the measures that precede and follow by chords built in perfect fourths—creating what we now refer to as a "modal" sound.

Played as they are here over a pedal point, these quartal harmonies are an early version of the piano style made famous by McCoy Tyner during his performing and recording days with the late John Coltrane. One needs only to add a pentatonic scale in the treble to get the right effect:

Using a less modal approach, pianist Bill Evans made use of these Gershwinesque voicings for much of his performing life, as in this brief example from his improvisation on the song "Emily."

MY MAN'S GONE NOW

Arranged by JED DISTLER

Words by DU BOSE HEYWARD
Music by GEORGE GERSHWIN

71

Pianist/composer Jimmy Rowles haunting tune, The Peacocks (featured in the film 'Round Midnight') also appears in this book. Rowles has performed with many greats over the years, including Lester Young, Billie Holiday, Benny Goodman, Les Brown, Tommy Dorsey, Stan Getz, Charlie Parker, Zoot Sims and Chet Baker, in addition to a movie studio stint at 20th Century Fox, and, at one point, work for TV as well.

Asked to say something about the piece, Jimmy Rowles related this story: "I found a Wynton Kelly record called 'Kelly's Greats' in a record store and took it home. The playing absolutely knocked me out. Not only was Kelly fantastic, but Wayne Shorter was on the album, and his playing was just wonderful. Shortly after I went with Bill Holman to hear Art Blakey's group, which featured Wayne on saxophone. I ended up bringing Wayne Shorter and Cedar Walton back to my house after the gig. Wayne spotted the music to '502 Blues' on my piano and asked me to play it for him, and when I had finished he asked if he could have it to record on his next album. Of course I said yes.

"Years later I was with Zoot Sims in Brazil. We were standing in the lobby of a hotel when suddenly someone came up behind me and started humming '502 Blues.' 'Who are you?' I asked. 'Didn't you write that?' he responded. It turned out that he was a Brazilian pianist, and he took us to a piano and played my music for me. He was great! We ended up spending the whole evening with him."

502 BLUES

JIMMY ROWLES
(1918-   )

Jazz master George Shearing employs a similar harmonic device to the one used by Chopin, Jobim and others (see the article which appears with "How Sensitive") in this haunting arrangement of a George Benson hit. It also appears in the collection "The World's Best Piano Arrangements" (CPP/Belwin).

THE GENTLE RAIN

Arranged by GEORGE SHEARING

MATT DUBEY
LUIZ BONFA

75

Bllly Taylor's "Rejoice"— an analysis

by Michael Cochrane

Billy Taylor has been known to many for his ability communicate about the art of jazz improvisation. Among his be beliefs is the strong conviction th t jazz can be taught. Through the years Taylor, who received his Ph.D. in music education from the University of Massachusetts in 1975, has met the challenge of teaching musicians and listeners about jazz. He is the author of several instructional books on playing jazz. His book *Jazz Piano —History and Development* (Wm. C. Brown Company, 1982), based on his Ph.D. thesis, is a thorough look at the development of jazz piano from ragtime to fusion. The text is well illustrated with dozens of musical examples. Currently, he reaches the general public with his subtly educational television pieces for CBS's *Sunday Morning*. Taylor is a gifted pianist who, aside from leading his own trio for many years, has worked with many of the great jazz leaders such as Charlie Parker, Miles Davis, Dizzy Gillespie, Milt Jackson, and Art Blakey, to name a few. His style definitely reflects the bebop period. He has a very lyrical approach to phrasing solos. His touch is light and articulate. Taylor also has a beautiful harmonic approach.

"Rejoice", one of Taylor's compositions, is very bright in character. A brief look at this composition will shed light on some aspects of Taylor's style. "Rejoice" is written in 6/8 time. The form is as follows:

A	A	B	A´
8 bars	8 bars	8 bars	10 bars

The melody begins with a two-bar *motive* which *is sequenced* in the next two bars to form a four bar phrase. This is followed by another four bar phrase consisting of two two-bar *motifs*. Graphically, the *A* section would look like this:

4 bar phrase		4 bar phrase	
2 bar motive	2 bar sequence	2 bar motive	2 bar motive

8 bar period

The *B* section also consists of two four-bar phrases which form an eight-bar *period*. The cadence at the end of the *B* section moves the piece into a repeat of the *A* section. Of interest to me, in the *B* section, is the use of intervallic patterns formed by combining major seconds with perfect fourths (measures 11 and 13) and minor seconds and minor thirds (measure 15). These patterns add a certain tension to the bridge, contrasting it from the more lyrical *A* section.

The final *A´* section, with two bars added in measures 25 and 26, completes the form. Note the dotted quarter *harmonic rhythm* in the last four bars. The melodic movement is in dotted eighth notes—four attacks in each measure of 6/8 time. The four-against-six feeling propels the music to a climactic close.

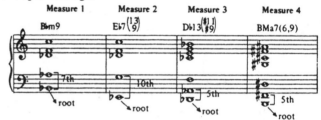

In the piano arrangement, the chords are voiced, primarily, in open position. My own definition of open position is as follows:

1) The root should appear in the bass 99% of the time.

2) The note directly above the root should form the interval of a fifth, seventh or tenth.

3) The overall spread of the chord spaces the intervals widely at the bottom and more closely at the top. Here are examples of Taylor's open voicings.

Taylor has formed many of the chords in this piece in open position. As you play the chords, notice the rich, warm, resonant sound quality of each. The harmony definitely adds color and depth to the composition as a whole.

Billy Taylor performs "Rejoice" on a recording entitled *Let Us Make a Joyful Noise*. The trio plays the piece somewhat faster than it is marked in the score. I found the metronome setting to be J. = 84mm. The quicker tempo generates a happy quality to the piece, hence the title "Rejoice." Taylor's playing is nimble and surefooted, and his performance, here and throughout . . . A *Joyful Noise*, is surely a lesson for all.

Pianist Michael Cochrane teaches jazz piano at NYU.

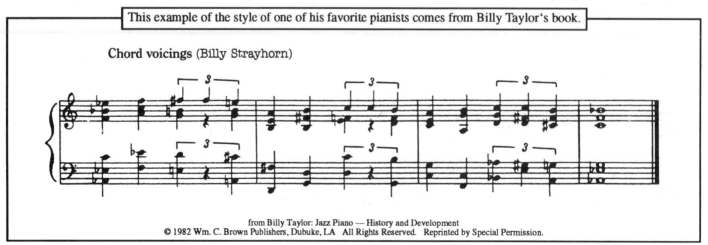

This example of the style of one of his favorite pianists comes from Billy Taylor's book.

Chord voicings (Billy Strayhorn)

REJOICE

BILLY TAYLOR
(1921-   )

* alternatively F#6,9/E

The Billy Taylor Trio plays the suite *Let Us Make Joyful Noise*, including "Rejoice," on an audio cassette available from
Betco Records, Box 630184, Bronx, NY 10463-9994.

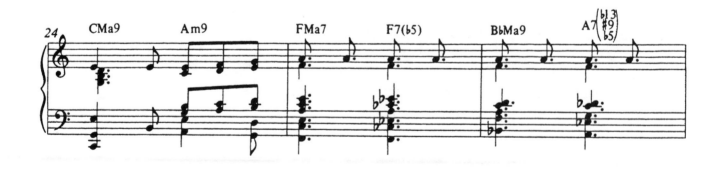

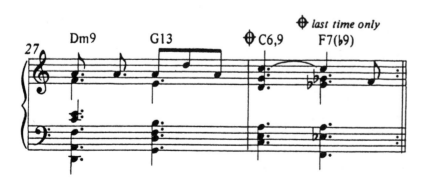

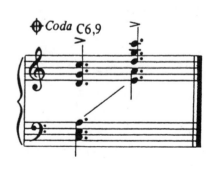

78

GEORGIA ON MY MIND

as recorded by Thomas "Fats" Waller in 1941 on RCA (BS63887-1)

Transcribed by BECCA PULLIAM

HOAGY CARMICHAEL
STUART GORRELL

79

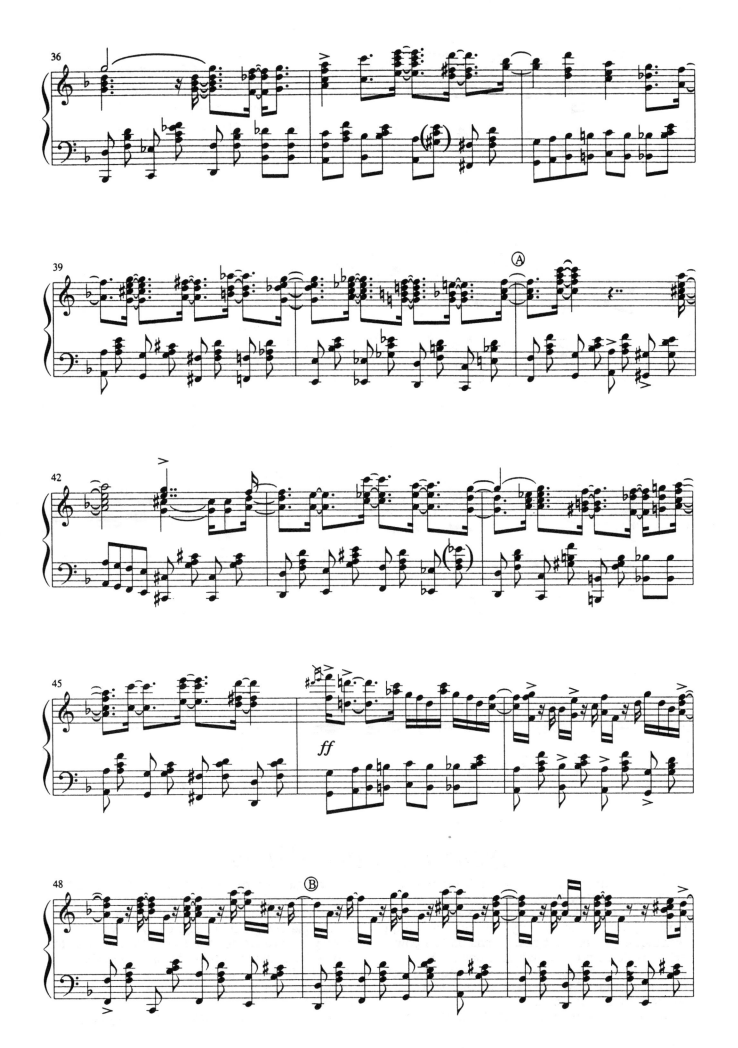

Notes on "Fats" Waller

"That Tatum," Thomas Waller is quoted as saying in the New York *Times* in 1939, "he was just too good and it looked like they were running him out of the city. He had too much technique. When that man turns on the powerhouse don't no one play him down. He sounds like a brass band . . . subdued and not blatant. None of this boogie woogie stuff that's just monotonous."

Waller used the occasion to go on about boogie woogie. He disliked it. A clause in all his contracts prohibited linking the term "boogie woogie" with the name "Fats" Waller.

"Boogie woogie is all right if you want to beat your brains out for five minutes. But for more than that you have to have melody. Jimmie Johnson taught me that. You got to hang onto the melody and never let it get boresome."

Melody gets secondary attention in boogie

woogie. The trademark of the style is an unflagging, propulsive, strong and steady left hand pattern extended over the form of the song. In the World War I era, James P. "Jimmie" Johnson advanced a new and different left hand style – stride – a swinging, modernized ragtime. His left hand was rhythmically dependable but deliciously varied in other aspects. All stride piano players to come would be judged against him. Yet even Johnson seemed to defer to Waller when he said of his former pupil, "His left hand was superior. A perfect left hand!"

In 1932, he had his own radio program as "the harmful little armful" on WLW Cincinnati. The CBS network brought him to New York for a regular 9AM program. "I used to have to stay up all night to make it," said Fats. Besides his extroverted piano playing, Waller's personality and sly humor made him a great catch for a radio network. He also appeared in some films.

Waller studied with Carl Bohm and Leopold Godowski – renowned classical teachers. His study with James P. Johnson was more pertinent to his professional life. Riccardo Scivales writes, "Waller was like a son to James P. Johnson."

"He dreamed of being a classical concert pianist, but his race prevented him from realizing his career," Scivales writes in the book *Harlem Stride Piano Solos*. "His audience and recording companies appreciated him mainly for his singing and his bulky figure. For this reason, from 1934 to 1943 [the year of his death] he recorded hundreds of songs singing and leading combos (His Rhythm) and reworking popular tunes (most of low musical quali-

ty) . . . . He took his revenge by desecrating them. Waller's sharp irony and iconoclastic *double-entendres* mocked the sickening sentimentalism of this kind of song. . . .

"This . . . phase of his artistry resulted in some masterwork recordings, however, such as 'Georgia on My Mind.'"

The electrifying "Georgia"

"Georgia," as played by Waller for the 1941 RCA session, opens with a *rubato* chorus. Our transcription (pages 16-18) begins with the second chorus. As David Thomson writes in liner notes to the *Time-Life Giants of Jazz* reissue of the 1941 disc, "Waller slides into tempo on the second chorus and takes it, literally, in stride. . . . he has a little fun on the bridge. . . . For the last chorus, he introduces a favorite trick of stride pianists, keeping the melody in the same tempo while switching to double time in the left hand; the effect is electrifying." It is also very difficult to execute, and thoroughly daunting at Waller's tempo. But "Fats" makes it sound almost easy.

In 1942, the year before his death, Waller performed at Carnegie Hall. (This was not the only time.) A reviewer wrote, "The concert was one of those long, easy-going, immensely entertaining events, with Fats Waller performing with equal success on the piano and Hammond organ. Principal items on the program were his songs, selected at random and with the utmost informality from a printed list of no less than 91, covering a span of 22 years."

As Art Tatum often said, "Fats Waller: that's where I come from!"

The notes on the CD reissue of this cut give the historical perspective: "With the release of his single 'Georgia on My Mind," Ray Charles turned a Hoagy Carmichael standard into his own anthem of pain and longing. This daring artistic move stuck gold with the public and climbed straight to #1 on the Billboard charts in 1960. " Jeffrey Todd Cohen sent us a reduction of the score with the note: "Ray Charles' tasteful, timeless arrangement and production make lt a most revered and durable cinch for a time capsule. It has such sturdy 'legs' that, after months of attempting to transcribe the score (high and low strings, piano, lead and background vocal),

I was no less intrigued than I had been upon my first hearing during my childhood. "

We reduced it further, to a vocal/piano excerpt, with adjustments to show a keyboard figure from the second chorus in the first. After bar 16 strings swell and overwhelm the piano. The excerpt shown here best reveals the relationship between voices and piano, and the rhythmic subtleties. The piano is really spare! The artist's style encompasses country, gospel, blues, and even New Orleans influences (Charles worked there early in the 1950's)."Mr. Charles' version is 100% fat free," says Cohen.

GEORGIA ON MY MIND

Adapted by JEFFREY TODD COHEN
& BECCA PULLIAM

HOAGY CARMICHAEL
STUART GORRELL

Playing The Music Of "Bud" Powell

By Andy LaVerne

Any pianist playing modern jazz today is a musical descendant of "Bud" Powell, and I am certainly no exception. My very first jazz piano influences were Thelonious Monk, and later Bill Evans. For quite some time I was actually unaware of Bud's pianistic prowess, and his influence on the world of jazz piano. My musical mentors, however, had done my homework for me, as they were both inexorably tied to Bud's musical conception. Monk was a contemporary of Bud's, and early on in his career he actually took Bud under his wing. If you listen to early recordings of Bill Evans, you might be surprised at how much Bill sounds like Bud. As a matter of fact, you can easily trace Bill's solo piano conception to that of the bebop pioneer.

A few years ago, I decided to go to the source myself, and began an in-depth study of the music of Bud Powell. What I found was that although Bud possessed monstrous chops, his playing was devoid of frills and clichés, and always had great clarity, even while playing the driving, intricate lines associated with bebop. Bud pioneered the bebop piano style, which is characterized by strong linear right hand lines, and sparse, syncopat-

> ## Although Bud possessed monstrous chops, his playing was devoid of frills and clichés.

ed left hand chord voicings, which many times consisted of only roots and "guide tones" — thirds, and sevenths.

This was a sharp departure from the previous era of jazz piano, which had a much more active left hand (as in stride piano), and a more diatonic, less sophisticated right. One of the common criticisms leveled at Bud's bebop piano style was that he had "no left hand." One infamous night at Birdland, Bud responded to these critics by playing the entire night with only his left hand! Ironically, Bud's idol, Art Tatum, had one of the most facile left hands in the history of jazz piano and at a very early age Bud was able to replicate anything he heard Tatum play.

My search into Bud's music has led to many interesting projects, the first of which was a Jazz Fellowship I received in 1989 from the National Endowment for the Arts. I presented a concert at New York's Cami Hall, playing the music of Bud Powell. More recently, I completed a solo piano recording on the SteepleChase label of Bud's music, simply titled "Bud Powell." The title

tune is a piece written by Chick Corea, himself a great admirer of Bud. In a few weeks, I am recording some of these same tunes for the Yamaha PianoSoft label (to be played on the Yamaha Disklavier). This project's title tune is "In Walked Bud," written by none other than Thelonious Monk.

All three of the aforementioned projects feature my arrangement of Bud's original, "Hallucinations," presented in this issue. This arrangement contains sections as played originally by Bud himself, notably the last four measures of the tune, often referred to as the "send off." I have added some of my own voicings and phrasing to give it a more personal stamp. I quickly learned by playing all this Bud Powell music that I am much more comfortable playing my own interpretations rather than trying to sound just like Bud. This of course, is what the tradition of jazz is all about: to assimilate various influences in order to create your own style — just as Bud did! ∎

Earl "Bud" Powell

The bebop period was a time of swirling lines, break-neck tempos, and new experiments that tested the limits of harmonic structure. But it also gave birth to countless tales of personal tragedy — of broken hearts, of drugs, and of too much talent with not enough self-respect. No one symbolizes that era like Bud Powell.

He was born in New York City on September 27, 1924. His father William, a stride pianist, says that when Bud was just seven "musicians would come and actually steal him, take him from place to place playing music. Nobody had ever seen a jazz musician that young. By the time he was ten he could play everything he'd heard by Fats Waller and Art Tatum." Bud left school at fifteen, but soon came under the tutelage of Thelonious Monk, who brought him to the bandstand at Minton's, where Bud got to play with Charlie Christian and Charlie Parker. Soon he was making recordings with Cootie Williams, who became his guardian. In 1943 Dizzy Gillespie formed a group with Bird, Don Byas, Max Roach and Oscar Pettiford, and slotted Bud as the pianist. But Powell was underage, and Cootie wouldn't let him go.

At the age of twenty-one he was arrested for disorderly conduct; a month later he entered the first of many mental institutions. Throughout his life he was often hospitalized, with treatment ranging from electro-shock therapy to beatings and dousings with ammoniated water. His explosive temperament created problems on and off the bandstand. Trumpeter Fats Navarro once attempted to smash Bud's hands with his horn; Charlie Parker fought with him on the stage of Birdland.

In 1959 Bud moved to Paris where he was enthusiastically received. His companion of that time, François Paudras, stated that Powell was not crazy or lost but "in a state of grace." Nevertheless, Bud Powell died on August 1, 1966 from tuberculosis, alcoholism and malnutrition. Five thousand people lined the streets of Harlem to mourn his passing.

—Stuart Isacoff

HALLUCINATIONS

Arranged by ANDY LaVERNE

EARL "BUD" POWELL

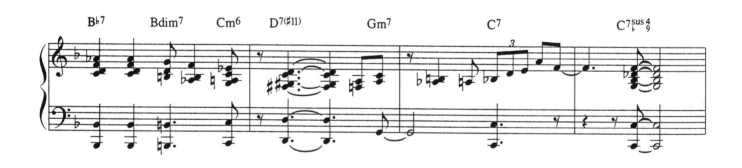

Bud Powell's Improvisation
On "Hallucinations"

An Excerpt
Transcribed by Bob Himmelberger

89

Creating Variety:
George Cables' "Helen's Song"

By Robert Ricci

A fascinating aspect of musical composition concerns the question of how variety is achieved within the boundaries of a piece, and how the musical elements of repetition and imitation serve to unify. Every piece of music in every style, whether it be on a large or small scale, must confront these musical considerations. In the jazz idiom, since more often than not the dimensions tend to be more restricted compositionally to allow for improvisation, the importance of variety as it interacts with compositional stability takes on an even more pronounced emphasis.

The much heralded jazz pianist George Cables, a veteran of groups led by such luminaries as Freddy Hubbard, Dexter Gordon, Art Pepper, Bud Shank, Max Roach and Sonny Rollins to mention but a few, has come into his own as leader and composer in more recent years. His facile technique, creative harmonic sense (in particular his use of diminished scale and chord devices) coupled with a remarkable sense of swing and explosive pyrotechnical runs, have made him one of the top pianists in jazz today.

His upbeat Latin-flavored composition, "Helen's Song," lends itself well to a discussion of repetition and contrast within the confines of a work. The piece is rather static at the outset, utilizing parallel triadic movement in the introduction as it then proceeds to employ close parallel D major voicings at A. The primary tonality through measure eight is a pedal D major with a touch of B minor.

This area serves as a level of harmonic stability or plateau. Beginning in measure nine the harmonic rhythm is accelerated and the chordal colors change considerably from the more static ones found initially. One is prepared psychologically for this change by the opening musical stability which then tends to enhance the harmonic momentum of this phrase.

Note that the melody also becomes more active in measure nine, although Cables employs some of the identical rhythmic syncopation found in earlier measures. In this way an element from the start of the piece is carried forth into a different musical setting — in a sense, something old and something new. Similarly, the reuse of syncopated parallel triads in measures eighteen through twenty are reminiscent of the triads in the piece's introduction.

The changes for improvisation, which are set off by a strong D7+9 dominant, are, like the piece itself, plateau-like at the outset, involving four measure spans of G minor moving to D major. Note that a minor cast sets off this section from the predominant major cast of the tune. The contrasting phrases with accelerated harmonic motion then reappear.

In a rubato-like coda at C the material found earlier at measure 9 undergoes a harmonic transformation as it is extended through a cycle of fifth chord changes, unlike the earlier section. The piece then ends in rubato fashion employing the parallel triadic material from the early part of the composition.

Hence, a consummate balance is achieved in "Helen's Song" through the musical devices of repetition, contrast, modification and imitation. They are truly elements and principles of great musical construction in every piece worth remembering. ∎

HELEN'S SONG

GEORGE CABLES

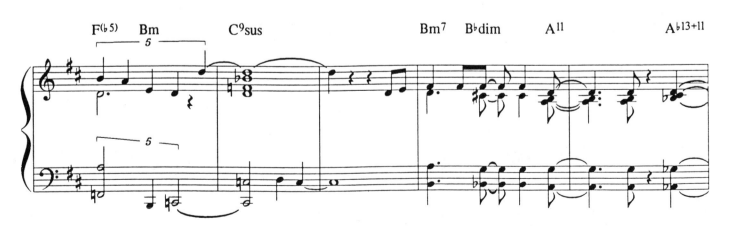

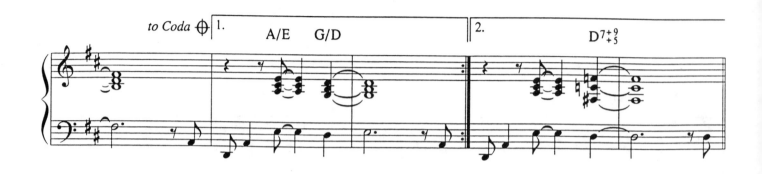

92

HERE'S THAT RAINY DAY

Arranged by ANDY LaVERNE

JIMMY VAN HEUSEN
JOHNNY BURKE

Special thanks to Jerry Bergonzi — A.L.

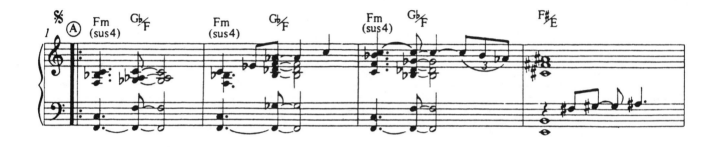

 In this arrangement, Andy has used simplified chord symbols — no extensions or alterations beyond the seventh — because he feels that you're more likely to be given basic chord symbols in a working situation. You would add your own coloration to the chords and the modes you choose for improvising.

He suggests that you play over and over on the introduction, with the left hand voiced in fourths

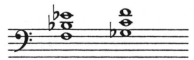

and the right hand improvising on the F Phrygian scale.

Modes for further improvising:
measure 4 — E Lydian for F#/E.

measure 5 and following — Dorian for minor chords, either Lydian or Ionian for majors, Mixolydian for dominant sevenths.

altered dominants — to fit the voicings, such as in measure 7 where the B7 contains ♭5 and ♭9, try the altered dominant scale.

measure 8 — try the A7(alt) scale.

95

Noreen Sauls has taken a cue from Chopin — and Antonio Carlos Jobim — in this bossa nova arrangement, based on the harmonic device used by both. (See her article following this piece of music.)

HOW SENSITIVE

NOREEN SAULS
FREDERIC CHOPIN

Bossa nova

Vamp interlude

1st time only   2nd time only   *Repeat and fade to end*

Chromatic Alteration Of Static Harmonies

BY NOREEN SAULS

In his book Jazz Keyboard, musician/educator Jerry Coker refers to a harmonic device that is used often in pop and jazz harmony; Coker describes it with the term "Contrapuntal Elaboration of Static Harmony." This simply means that one voice of a chord is in motion (contrapuntal elaboration), while the others are not (static). You're probably familiar with many tunes that use this approach. Think of the James Bond theme, with the fifth of the chord moving chromatically while the root remains stationary.

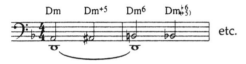

Or of the way Ellington has the root of a minor triad descend in half steps on "In A Sentimental Mood."

The same device occurs in "My Funny Valentine," with a C minor harmony.

Of course, this kind of movement has it origins in much earlier music, such as Chopin's famous E minor Prelude, which Antonio Carlos Jobim used as the basis for his beautiful bossa nova, "How Insensitive." If we examine bars 2-8 of Chopin's original manuscript, extensive use of this harmonic movement can be found in the left hand.

I've taken the Chopin/Jobim harmonic pattern — with some updated, jazzier chord voicings —to create the bossa nova on the next page. Here are some comments on the piece, with suggestions for ways to excerpt the devices used so that you can apply them to other playing situations.

At letter A, the bottom voice provides rhythmic drive and some subtle harmonic movement. Otherwise, the original Chopin voicings were maintained. Letter B find the harmonies opening up and stretching out. From letter C on you'll find an improvisation.

Bars 5 and 6 of letter C are an example of "contrapuntal elaboration" of a static harmony — perhaps more accurately entitled "chromatic alteration." Only the second voice from the top is moving, as the chord changes from Dm9 to Dmin-maj7, Dm9 and, finally, Dm69. Practice these voicings in all keys.

In bars 17-18 of letter C, the right hand features a melodic pattern over a ii-V progression (in this case, Dm7-G7), which may come in handy in your own improvisations. Try transposing this to other keys also. Bars 26, 28 and 30 illustrate the use of yet another device, tri-tone harmonies: a D Flat chord in the right hand against a G7 in the left; a C in the right hand against an F#7 in the left; and B and F chords in the right hand against an F7 in the left. You can make an exercise out of this technique for future use (there are 6 possible pairs of matched tritones). The following example is just one idea.

As you study this arrangement, look for other ideas to extract and apply elsewhere, such as voicings, melodic lines, and rhythms. ∎

99

Bill Evans' Chord Changes on *"I Fall In Love Too Easily"*

BY JACK REILLY

A reharmonization of any standard chord progression should replace the original chords with something better. The term "better" could be defined in many ways, of course: as more interesting, more dissonant, more consonant, or as giving one the "feeling" of roving into another region (key). In other words, there must be a sound reason for choosing the reharmonization and it must not destroy the melodic tension or drama, but rather, it must enhance it. This is a very demanding task, and one must be aware of all the possibilities, those obvious and those not so.

This article will take you step by step through the progression of "I Fall In Love Too Easily," in order to shed some light on Bill Evans' thought processes with regard to the choice of a "better" chord, and to gain more insight into this fascinating and much-maligned or abused subject, reharmonization.

The first step is to determine what other regions are suggested or can be suggested by the original progression. Most of the standard tunes that are part of the jazz musician's repertoire were written before 1950 and are, therefore, very diatonic, i.e. they modulate or suggest keys (regions) that are closely related to the original key.

This tune is in the key of G Major. That means the closely related keys are D Major and C Major, and their three relative minors: E minor, B minor and A minor. The secondary dominants are A7, G7, B7, F#7 and E7. The term "secondary dominant" is another way of saying "the fifth of." A7 is the fifth of D Major; G7 is the fifth C Major; B7 is the fifth of E minor; F#7 is the fifth of B minor; and E7 is the fifth of A minor. These secondary dominants have the ability to destroy or weaken the original key.

When we alter these chords, i.e. flat the fifth, add a ninth, raise the fifth, etc., we give them more power and energy (dissonance) and further weaken the key center or tonic, but strengthen a new one. Composer Arnold Schoenberg teaches us that the VII, III+5 and IIo chords can also <u>function</u> like a secondary dominant, that is, weaken the original key center and/or enrich the diatonic progression. The VII chord is diminished, the III+ is augmented and the IIo is half-diminished; these are dissonant (active) chords. The IIo and III+ belong to the minor scale. The VII chord is half-diminished in both major and minor, but is a full diminished only in the minor scale.

Bill Evans used these principles in this reharmonization — the new chords are "borrowed from" one of the diatonic regions of the original.

The chords in measures 3 and 5, for example, belong to the region of E minor and prepare the arrival of the modulation to the relative minor of G Major at measure 9. The E minor key then functions as the dominant minor of A minor which arises in measure 12. The final phrase (beginning at measure 13) jumps to the relative major (C) of A minor to begin the descent to G Major via two secondary dominants, B7 and E7 in measure 14.

The turn-around (measure 16) is the most interesting measure for me: every quarter note pulse has a substitute chord. On the downbeat, instead of the I (tonic chord), we get the VIIo7 of D Major; beat two is a Cm7, the only non-diatonic chord in the entire progression. It's borrowed from the key of G minor, the parallel minor, three fifths removed from the original key. On the third beat, Bill uses the perfect substitute for a tonic chord, the III7, Bm7. And on the fourth beat, Bill places his favorite tension chord, a secondary dominant seventh, flat nine, plus nine, augmented eleventh chord built on the second degree of the G Major scale. Most fake books would label it a Bbo7 chord. That is misleading and does not give us any real insight into why this chord functions the way it does. It's an altered II chord, functioning as a secondary dominant on its return to the dominant region of the key in measure 1.

In the second ending, Bill creates the feeling of a tag or extension by the use of secondary dominants, again, borrowed from the diatonic regions of A minor and B minor. And as a complete surprise, he ends the tune with a super-powerful progression — II7, I7 (Am7 to GMa7) — with a brilliant idea: to make a cadenza on the Am7. When I play this tune, I end on EMa7 in the final measure instead of GMa7. The Am7 then functions as a IV minor chord of E Major, creating the "feel" of a plagal cadence: IV (A minor) to I (E Major). ∎

This article is adapted from the book The Harmony Of Bill Evans *by Jack Reilly, available through Unichrom Publishing Company, 125 Prospect Park West, Brooklyn, NY 11215.*

─I FALL IN LOVE TOO EASILY─

Reharmonization by JACK REILLY

Words by SAMMY CAHN
Music by JULE STYNE

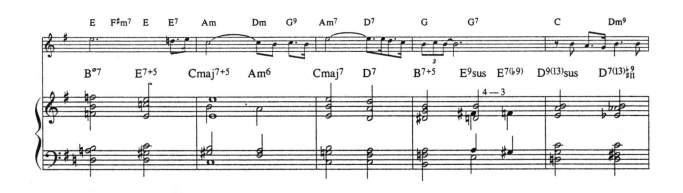

101

Getting to know "Ill Wind"

Noreen Sauls

Recordings brought "Ill Wind" to me. Although I was in trumpeter Howard McGhee's band from 1979 through the early 80's, we never played one of my favorite pieces on his LP *The Sharp Edge* (Trio label) — "Ill Wind." Billie Holiday's version was my introduction to the wonderful lyric. I decided to make the piece part of my piano/vocal repertoire. Finally, I discovered Phineas Newborn's rendition on the album *Back Home* (Contemporary) and felt compelled to transcribe it.

I had the good fortune to see and hear Phineas perform in New York several times. He was a small, energetic man, possessing amazing technical facility and the ability to draw an endless variety of colors from the piano. His playing is exceptionally "clean," making the runs relatively easy to transcribe, as long as you can negotiate his speed!

Newborn begins the piece in a solo piano style for the first chorus. He then merges with bass and drums for some improvisation, before ending the piece alone. The middle section is abridged in our presentation. The ideal performance guide is the recording, but it has not been reissued on CD. If you're not familiar with the standard, get the sheet music. The song form is not the standard 32 bars; both *A* and *B* sections are longer. It's tempting to shorten them, but the song becomes less haunting without them.

Phineas Newborn's solo style

The salient feature is the use of fills in both hands. The right hand runs in mm. 2-3 and 17 are not so difficult as they first appear. A melodic sequence is repeated, octave after octave, ascending.

When large, unreachable intervals appear, especially in the left hand, just roll them and use a light pedal. You may want to use this technique in mm. 10, 14, 16-17.

The left hand pattern at *B* (mm. 19-20, 23-24) is very useful to get from **I** to **IV**. The **D** chord alone could suffice for these two measures, but the added passing chords create movement and variety. Practice the progression in all keys, and you'll find many applications for it in other tunes.

One of the pianist's trademarks appears in bar 35 — a two-handed unison pattern with the hands three octaves apart. This device is effective for fills or improvisation and contrasts with the heavier sound of full harmonies. Practice other patterns and fast-moving melodies (such as Charlie Parker tunes) with hands in unison and one, two, three *or more* octaves apart. Your left hand will probably lag at first, but practice will improve it rapidly. Use a metronome and work slowly. Comfortable, logical fingerings help too.

Concerning fingerings: please practice the traditional scales and arpeggios in all major and minor keys. These exercises are your best guide to fingering other patterns. The fingerings shown in the transcription will get you started. If something doesn't feel comfortable, change it.

The final step in learning this transcription involves harmonic/melodic analysis. Write in the chord changes and try to relate each melodic pattern to a particular chord, scale or arpeggio. Thorough analysis helps you set up other tunes in a solo style.

Because this is *rubato* in tempo, you can take your time. Make use of *accelerandi*, *ritards*, and dynamics for dramatic effect. This flexibility allows you to slow down for hard passages and speed up for easy ones. Newborn's freedom with time suggests that he is doing the same — tossing off phrases of familiar melody and more carefully executing spur-of-the-moment, original flourishes. Even if he played it a thousand times, this is the illusion of spontaneity he creates.

ILL WIND

as played by Phineus Newborn, Jr., on Back Home *(Contemporary C-7648)*

Transcribed by NOREEN SAULS
with BECCA PULLIAM

Lyric by TED KOEHLER
Music by HAROLD ARLEN

104

105

106

Tatum and Hancock blow on "Ill Wind"

Becca Pulliam

"Ill Wind (You're Blowin' Me No Good)" is an easy song to play wrong. The refrain has an *AABA* form, but it is not 32 measures in length; it's 40. This is the form:

A1	10 mm
A2	10 mm
B	8 mm
A3	12 mm

The full original version is available in *The Harold Arlen Songbook*, published by MPL Communications and distributed by Hal Leonard Publishing.

Art Tatum displays a delicious variety of colorful figures and creative harmony on his solo "Ill Wind" (Pablo 2310-789-A). He reharmonizes the *A*-strain tails with II-V sequences or chord progressions that descend chromatically. He fills sustained melodic notes with inner voices, played in parts by both hands. His single-note fills can tumble straight down, hook slightly at the top and then fall, fall skittishly, or swirl. Listening to one swirly figure, I'm sure I heard boughs of leaves tossed by fickle winds.

"Behind-the-beat phrasing is a technique that communicates jazz feeling to a standard."

For a reharmonized "Ill Wind" that may be inspired by Tatum, see John Mehegan's *Jazz Improvisation 1* book.

On the album *Cornbread* (Blue Note 784-222-2), trumpeter Lee Morgan and pianist Herbie Hancock do something very special

Herbie Hancock two-bar pattern introduces Lee Morgan's "Ill Wind"

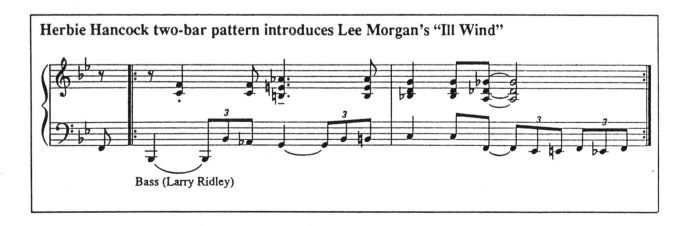

Bass (Larry Ridley)

with the form. A two-bar pattern, played four times, introduces the piece. This pattern recurs naturally as mm. 7-8 of *A1*, then is repeated to extend *A1* to ten measures. *A2* is the conventional eight, but *A3* includes six additional bars — the two-bar pattern played three times. Total of measures equals 40.

A1	10 mm
A2	8 mm
B	8 mm
A3	14 mm

The quintet chooses a relaxed, leisurely tempo. Morgan relaxes more, playing the melody way behind the beat. Sing the melody as written along with the recording, and you'll find the trumpeter is following you. Behind-the-beat phrasing is a technique that communicates jazz feeling to a standard.

Hancock's 32-bar, one-chorus solo has some blues phrases as well as a quote from "It Might As Well Be Spring." The feeling intensifies toward quarter-note triplet, high register block chords at the end of *B*. Then Hancock relaxes the thickness but increases the motion as he spins off sixteenth-note runs on the last *A*. His tone has a quality that matches the muted trumpet. ●

"In a Mist"—a new transcription of Bix Beiderbecke's 1927 piano solo

Bix Beiderbecke was a cornetist, composer, and occasional pianist who migrated from Davenport, Iowa, to the east coast at the height of the roaring twenties and barely survived them. To his young fans, many of them concentrated in Ivy League and other colleges, he apparently became a symbol of the conflicting currents of the jazz age. Upon the reissuing of a comprehensive selection of Bix Beiderbecke recordings, John J. Maloney reflected on the artist in the New York *Times* (May 11, 1952).

Bix was a creature of myth long before he died, and he died at 28. In his intelligent and informative program notes, George Avakian says that Bix lived in a 'Scott Fitzgerald atmosphere.' Actually, Bix did much more than merely live in a Fitzgerald atmosphere; in many ways he was the Fitzgerald of jazz. ~'Like Scott, Bix came from a well-to-do, middle-class, middle-western family. He was as ignorant musically as Scott was about literary things (Bix had as much trouble reading notes as Fitzgerald had trying to spell correctly.) A flagrant and compulsive waste scarred their lives. In order to get money they were forced to squander their energy doing cheap things— Bix playing with the big commercial bands and Scott grinding out stories for the slick magazines, and yet each was always rescued from mediocrity by the brief beautiful moment of genius....

"...alternating strains of semiclassical melody and modern French harmonies, against jazz stomping..."

"Eventually, both became appalled by how much they felt they didn't know, in an academic sense, about their respective crafts, and they began to explore—Bix, classical music, and Scott, the classics. Yet, in spite of all the searching, they remained 'in a mist,' seeking the ineffable, living beyond their physical and emotional means; and the magnificent paradox is that each of these bankrupts managed to produce the most disciplined work of his gaudy era . . ."

Beiderbecke memorial societies, gatherings at his grave, and devotion to his recordings were still reported forty and fifty years after his short, brilliant career. In the U.S. and Britain, at least three biographies have been published.

Beiderbecke recorded the piano solo "In a Mist" on September 9, 1927. His peers recognized the striking harmonic, stylistic, and formal qualities of this unusual recording; but those closest to Beiderbecke were not at all surprised at its individuality. One biographer and disciple Ralph Berton, (*Remembering* Bix was published by Harper and Row in 1974), remembers the moment when he and Beiderbecke first listened to "In a Mist" together. Berton writes, "Oh, it was feeble, stiff, self-conscious, compared to what I'd heard him do hundreds of times in our living room— pale stuff for Bix, but . . . instantly, unmistak-

ably [him] . . . ! . . . alternating strains of modest semiclassical melody and modern French harmonies, against the dirty (sic) jazz stomping—Bix's familiar Jekyll-and-Hyde personality, complete with uncertain tempo and a few blurred fingertips."

Over several months, under the composer's careful supervision, Beiderbecke's musical associate William Challis (described by the biographer as "Bix's Boswell") created the written version of "In a Mist." It is not a transcription of the record. It includes an additional section unheard on the recording, and a theory explaining that discrepancy is that the original publisher wanted "In a Mist" to be as successful as Gershwin's "Rhapsody in Blue," so he encouraged imitation of the extended form. According to the current publisher (Columbia Pictures), the Beiderbecke/Challis sheet music is soon to go out of print.

Don Wilhite of Indiana whetted our interest in "In a Mist" by sending a full transcription of the original recording, one that proved faithful and accurate, and difficult to play! What appears here are the first 38 bars. Here is what Mr. Wilhite has to say about the piano solo.

Notes on "In a Mist"

The form of the piece is **ABCDA'E**. Each section is a conventional 16 bars. The Interlude serves as an introduction to **C** and **D**.

The pervasive sound of the whole tone scale is heard in each section. Whole tone chords ascend or descend with each voice moving to its next note by whole steps, requiring at least two adjacent chords for the sound. Unlike the sound of other contiguous chords, it is easily recognized because it is the same chord transposed, step by step, higher or lower. Section **B** poses a four-bar musical question in the guise of whole tone clusters, then answers the phrase with the "hot," syncopated style of the twenties in the likeness of a major tonality and chromaticisms.

Bix's ability to hear and play tension tones in his improvisations—unusual melodic tones which are not factors of the chord against which they are sounded—distinguished him from his colleagues. Until Bix came along, the solos of this period were "chord-minded," alluding to the players' preoccupation with the root, third, fifth, and seventh of the chord. It seems that they created melodies by an overcautious reference to the harmony.

Bix Beiderbecke was one of the first great jazzmen to use his natural gift of hearing in the utilization of tension tones. Although the tension points were used much earlier by French Impressionist composers, this device for both improvising and composing was unheard of until Bix and regarded as unconventional by the improvisers of his day.

Bix, with his great ear, was aware that his favorite Impressionist composers, Ravel and Debussy, had used these sensitive tones commonly in their writing. In addition, he had heard and absorbed the frequent use of the *augmented dominant ninth* in the jazz-oriented compositions of George Gershwin. It is no wonder, then, that he could hear tension notes above the conventional and single chords in the popular tunes of the twenties.

IN A MIST

as released on a Jazz Piano Trilogy (Columbia KG32355)

Transcribed by DON WILHITE

LEON "BIX" BEIDERBECKE
(1903-1931)

© **Interlude**

111

ISN'T IT ROMANTIC

as played on Bill Mays & Ray Drummond: One to One 2 *(dmp CD-482)*

Arranged by BILL MAYS

Music by RICHARD RODGERS
Lyric by LORENZ HART

113

Note from the arranger

"Isn't It Romantic?" is usually played in 4/4 and as a ballad, but I wanted to shed new light on this great old standard by putting it in a lilting 6/4 and altering it a lot harmonically. I kept the melody absolutely in tact. Next, I decided that I wanted the solo blowing to be in two different keys — half in D, half in E♭. I then wanted to "telegraph" that two-key thing in the melody statement of the song. Using an ascending and descending chromatic bass movement, bar 1 begins in the key of D and bar 5 seems to suggest E♭. (That happens again in bars 17 and 21.) This bitonal idea is carried out again in bars 31-33 and in the coda, with the last bar of the arrangement never deciding which of the two keys it's really in.

There's a lot of **IIIm-VI-IIm-V** harmonic movement inherent in the song, so to give it some "breathing space," I used some pedal A's and B♭'s in the soloing section, and the feeling should stay in "one" (as opposed to a walking six feel) most of the time. — *Bill Mays*

Shooting the rapids
with a young piano stylist

by Becca Pulliam

Midnight had passed. It was 1989. The coast-to-coast National Public Radio broadcast was over. The liquor was cleared from the tables at the Dakota Bar and Grill in St. Paul, Minnesota. But, to the delight of a few tables of early morning revelers, pianist Harry Connick, Jr. would not get off the stage!

Harry's been onstage since he was five. In his hometown — New Orleans — he used to sit in on Bourbon Street with musicians such as Buddy Rich. He was only nine when Rich invited him to go on tour. (Harry said no.) That's the same year that the child prodigy played "I'm Just

Photo by David Gahr   Harry Connick, Jr.

Wild about Harry" in a documentary with Eubie Blake — age 96 at the time.

This winter — his 22nd — has been hot for Harry Connick, Jr. An important New York engagement caught the attention of national media. In January, he began a month at the Oak Room of the sedate Algonquin Hotel. The critics and audiences loved him. He sold out 36 shows. He shot a TV special with fellow New Orleanian Dr. John and saxophonist Michael Brecker *and* a nine-foot Steinway together on the tiny Oak Room stage. *Time* and *Newsweek* noticed, and wrote about him in the same week. Immediately after that, he flew to Japan for more performances and excitement.

When he was 9, he played "I'm Just Wild about Harry" with Eubie Blake — age 96 at the time.

Throughout the sudden success, Connick has maintained an unaffected, comfortable stage presence. He speaks with a slight New Orleans drawl and a little local color, opening his Oak Room show by calling out, "Everybody say 'eh la bas!'" He does not hide his age; occasionally, on stage, he enjoys acting it. He has two albums of vintage songs that appeal to people born six decades before him, and he sings them with ease. But what really puts him over and makes him so phenomenal is his brilliant piano playing. As his hands heap one dazzling stylistic reference upon another, you might catch quick musical allusions to Art Tatum (runs), Erroll Garner (everything), the rambunctious stride of Fats Waller, and even fiery glissandos à la Jerry Lee Lewis.

Harry's piano is wonderfully entertaining and no less fun to analyze. During the Oak Room show, he did a bit in which he took the audience from Chicago to Kansas City to New Orleans, circa 1922. With his stomping foot as the "engine" he began in a Chicago speakeasy, playing the nimble boogie woogie of Meade Lux Lewis. Then, on the Kansas City stop, he played a walking bass and mimicked the minimal right hand style of Count Basie. Duke Ellington showed up! and — in a moment revealing Harry's great ear for subtle piano styles — he conducted an Ellington/Basie dialogue. The right hand began something like this:

Just as the audience quieted from hearty laughter to a chuckle over this routine, Oscar Peterson (born 1925) blew in, and the conversation went three-way. Harry added sixteenth-note outbursts to the sparse, sparkling comments of Basie and the middle-register phrases of Ellington.

Eventually, the train left Kansas City bound for New Orleans, a city with a piano tradition of its own. Jelly Roll Morton* was a founder. Harry also mentioned some key players from recent times — Professor Longhair and James Booker — men who never recorded on major labels but who exerted a tremendous in-person influence on all the postwar New Orleans musicians.

One of Harry's synthesized styles is to play songs from the twenties to the New Orleans beat. Harry credits this approach to his mentor, James Booker. For example, on his current record *Twenty*, he plays "Avalon" like this:

The left hand figure marks the beginning of the *clave* beat, an Afro-Cuban rhythmic pattern. It makes you want to dance. A little later in "Avalon," he expands his left hand figure into two others, and doubles the tempo.

"Avalon" is the opening cut on the album, and it became the show-stopping last number of his set at the Algonquin.

Practicing the transcription

The transcription of "Lazy River" on pages 1-3 shows Harry's stride style — so named because of the left hand's to and fro motion. Try to cultivate *slightly early* attacks in the left hand and *slightly late* ones in the right. This is ever so subtle. Give the right hand a little punch; the left is all background.

Harry mentions some key New Orleans players from recent times — Professor Longhair and James Booker . . .

We've abridged the record track to go from the end of the first chorus directly to the Erroll Garner finish. Don't play this too loudly. Make the tremolo chords shimmer. That's what Harry does. Every note in his flashy run rings out clearly. Try dividing the run between the hands, and don't let the tempo lag. Make it glitter!

It's a crowd-pleasing style in the hands of an irresistible new virtuoso, Harry Connick, Jr.●

LAZY RIVER

as played by Harry Connick, Jr., on Twenty *(CBS 44369)*

Transcribed and edited by BECCA PULLIAM

HOAGY CARMICHAEL
SIDNEY ARODIN

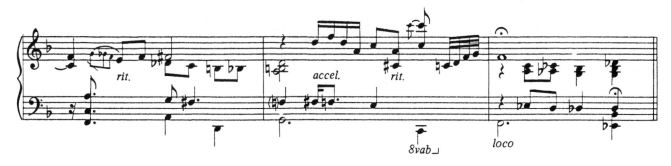

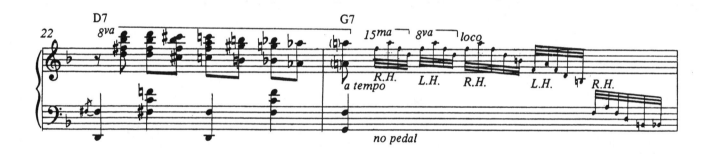

This transcription is abridged at mm. 18-19 to go directly from the opening chorus to the coda. Listen to the record to hear all the excitement in between.

IT COULD HAPPEN TO YOU

Arranged by BILL CHARLAP

JOHNNY BURKE & JIMMY VAN HEUSEN

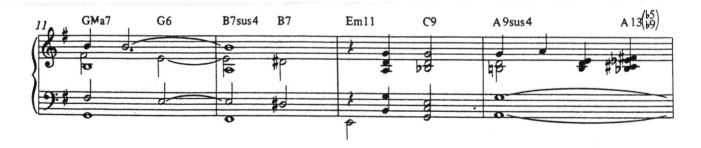

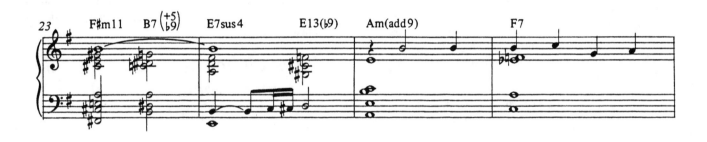

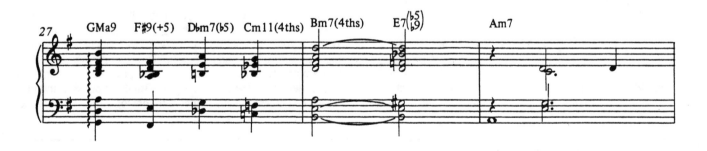

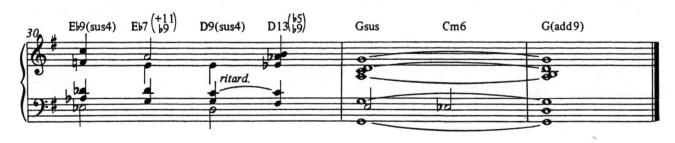

121

How to play stride piano— a lesson with Sir Roland Hanna

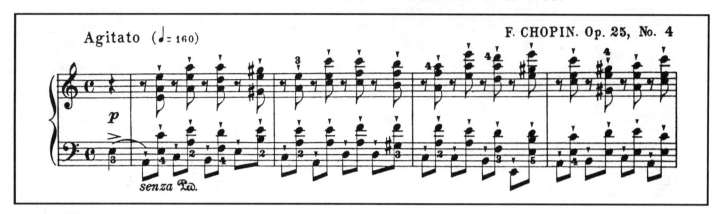

The word "stride" refers to the left hand technique that Sir Roland Hanna's composition employs elegantly. Hanna wrote the "Jazz Stride Etude" at a time when he was engaged in more teaching than he is today. Many of his students wanted to learn to play stride piano. At the time, he says he could suggest only the Chopin Etude in A Minor, Opus 2, Number 4.

In a conversation, Hanna gave us ideas about what you can learn from his "Jazz Stride Etude." "One of the lessons is how easy it is to play stride piano with single low notes or octaves alternating with chords in the left hand. And it's very useful. I use it, every night in solo playing.

"I used to give my students a systematic study of stride, alternating tenths and chords, two beats each. The progression would start simply in any key as a I-IV, and then explore the harmony of that key. The ambitious students would use chords outside the key to make the harmony more interesting. And I'd tell them to use any combinations they could think of, to increase their interest in stride playing. I also wrote the 'Jazz Stride Etude' about this time. "To learn the stride left hand, it should be played as if it were two separate parts. Practice the chords in a syncopated rhythm:

They should be learned so that you know exactly what each chord sounds like. Do this until you've memorized them. Then,

practice the other part, using the 'pinky' for the descending single notes. Finger the octaves (beginning in bar 9) with the thumb and fifth finger. Again, play staccato (separated), not legato (smoothly connected).

"When it comes to putting the two left hand parts together to play the stride, one should be very relaxed. Before you begin, let your arms dangle by your sides to get rid of all the tension. When your hand does strike the keyboard, maintain this relaxation and let the piano support the weight of your hand so you get a good tone. The piano should actually carry the weight of the hand landing on the keyboard. Even when you make mistakes, make them in a relaxed fashion!

"Even when you make mistakes, make them in a relaxed fashion!"

"You can use the pedal if you release it with every harmonic change: down on the low note, up on the chord. But it's best to work without the pedal, or to pedal only the wider skips, and also to arrive at as much legato as possible in the right hand without the pedal.

"As for the right hand part, you may follow the fingerings given or the alternate fingerings, but do vary the fingering over the course of your practice. When you work with an etude, varying the fingering makes the hand more flexible. It also gives your performance more flexibility. It's the mark of a 'pro' and I never met an amateur who didn't want to be a pro. "But don't put your thumb on a black key unless the other fingers follow logically. (For a black

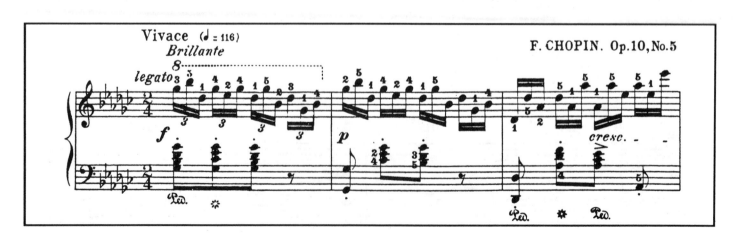

key etude, see the Chopin Etude in G♭, Opus 10, Number 5.) Another occasion for using the thumb on a black key is when you're sliding off a black key to an adjacent key—while playing the blues, for example. The thumb can take the punishment. But in this etude, I recommend keeping the thumb off the occasional black key. "Practice the right hand part in unison with both hands together. This will inspire different fingerings. Vary your touch from staccato to legato. The goal is to achieve a legato right hand without its becoming 'mushy.' It should be <u>crisp.</u> When you play the right hand an octave higher than it's written, it should <u>sparkle.</u>

"Eventually, strive to achieve a different quality from the piece each time you play it. That's what will give it 'etude' status for you.

"When I wrote it, I was thinking of the way Jelly Roll Morton (1885-1941) wrote for his band. The left hand chords would have been voiced by horns—trombones or saxophones. The low notes were played by the tuba (or later, the bass). A soloist on trumpet or clarinet or soprano sax would have played the right hand part. Some of Morton's melodies were harmonized by a second part. He was very meticulous about his writing."

Roland Hanna is one of the great Detroit-born jazz pianists. His father was a preacher in the Sanctified Church. As a child, Hanna studied classical music and was later influenced by his friend Tommy Flanagan to play jazz. He continued his education at the Eastman School of Music and Juilliard. A highlight of his career came in 1970 when he was knighted by the President of Liberia for educational and humanitarian work in Africa. Hanna's associations with the Thad Jones/ Mel Lewis Band and the New York Jazz Quartet are well documented. He has performed and recorded in Europe and Japan. For a solo recording, Hanna recommends <u>Swing Me No Waltzes</u> (Storyvllle 4018) from 1979.

A JAZZ STRIDE ETUDE

ROLAND P. HANNA
(1932-   )

JUST YOU, JUST ME

as played by Kenny Kirkland on Marian McPartland's Piano Jazz
in the style of Thelonious Monk

Transcribed by BECCA PULLIAM

JESSE GREEN
RAYMOND KLAGES
DAVE VOLPE

127

This up-tempo and challenging Ellington classic may also be heard on
"Dick Hyman Plays Duke Ellington" (Reference Recordings RR50 DCD).

JUBILEE STOMP

Arranged by DICK HYMAN

DUKE ELLINGTON

130

ON GREEN DOLPHIN STREET

Arranged by NOREEN SAULS

NED WASHINGTON
BRONISLAU KAPER

For ending — repeat last 2 measures and fade out.

Changing time feels

by Noreen Sauls

Noreen Sauls teaches jazz piano and leads a jazz choir at William Paterson College in New Jersey. She can also be heard performing with bassist Earl Sauls.

Just when you think you understand the difference between swing and a Latin feel, you will discover tunes that combine *both* styles. The key to playing these well is a transition so smooth that one time feel *melts* into the other. To explore this challenge, I've arranged the standard "On Green Dolphin Street" by Kaper and Washington.

This 32-bar tune is in an *ABAC* form. The repeated *A* section has a Latin feel, while *B* and *C* are in swing time. The most important element in this arrangement is the bass line. It *glues* the sections together gracefully.

The eight-bar introduction sets up the Latin feel, with a pedal point figure in the left hand and chromatically descending triads in the right. The first and second endings, on the other hand, feature a strong walking bass line and a more active melody. A hard driving swing prevails. The final two measures revert to Latin and can be used as a *fade-out* ending on the *out-head* (last chorus).

Drummers often handle this role . . . you can adapt some of their ideas.

Now, let's take a look at the important transitional measures where the time feel changes. In bar 16, just before the first ending, the *walking* bass sets up the swing feel for *B*. The intervals in the right hand (beats 2-4) rhythmically reinforce the bass line and prepare for the **Dm7** in bar 17.

The change back to Latin occurs in measure 24. With the bass still walking in quarter notes, the right hand — played in even eighth notes — sets up the Latin feel perfectly.

Three against four

This arrangement contains rhythmic combinations that may require some practice. Look at bars 10 and 14. The quarter note triplets in the right hand against the offbeats in the left will be hard to play at first. Practice this rhythm by breaking it down and playing it slowly, subdividing the beats to see how everything "lines up."

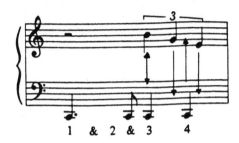

Look at beats 3 and 4 and picture the left hand rhythm as two quarter notes, as in the example above. This is simply a two-against-three rhythm. Play it until you feel comfortable.

Now, change beats 3 and 4 to four eighth notes. You have a three-against-four rhythm, as illustrated below.

If you subdivided the beats precisely, the last right hand note would slightly *precede* the "and" of beat 4. But when actually played this way, the figure has a "stiff" feeling. It is much more musical to be loose with the rhythm and almost *line up* the last two notes.

Once you're familiar with this tune, try others with changing time feels, such as "I'll Remember April," "Star Eyes," "Nica's Dream," and "A Night in Tunisia." Listen to how other musicians handle the time feel transitions. Drummers often handle this role, so perhaps you can adapt some of their ideas. With patient practice, you'll be making smooth transitions in no time! ●

A Fourth Chord Primer

BY ROBERT RICCI

After the release of the famous Miles Davis album "Kind of Blue" in 1959, the use of chord voicings utilizing fourths (Quartal structure) became increasingly popular, primarily due to the parallel "So What" chords used by Bill Evans.

Bill Evans

The second chord creates a Dm7 or Dm7(sus4) sound, as all of the notes are derived from a D Dorian scale. All intervals in these voicings are perfect fourths from the bottom up, with the exception of the major third on top. It is worth noting that chords constructed entirely of perfect fourths, unlike chords in thirds (tertian), tend to convey a sense of harmonic ambiguity, especially as more fourths are added. This can sometimes be a useful quality, as in many works by composer Paul Hindemith, when interval harmonic definition is not desired. In jazz, chords voiced in straight perfect fourths can hence convey either a major or minor quality, depending upon the root supplied.

Sometimes, for reasons of color, other notes may be added to the fundamental fourth structure—usually decorative sounds to a chord's primary members, or major thirds on top.

With a slight alteration of one or more of the perfect fourths, usually to an augmented fourth, other colors can be created that are most useful to the jazz pianist, particularly for major chord types.

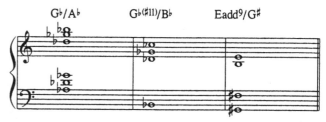

Dominant chord functions can likewise utilize fourth structures, but due to the tritone aspect of the dominant seventh sound, an augmented fourth is virtually mandatory, usually as the lowest interval. Rootless voicings are common for this type of quartal structure.

Quartal chords can convey a pedal effect nicely, but again some internal intervallic modification may be needed. In the three chords found below a perfect fifth is found internally, an augmented fourth is at the top of the second chord, and the third chord has a minor seventh as the lowest interval.

Quartal structures may also function as a lower fulcrum above which triads may be superimposed, a technique that lends itself to parallel motion, so common to the sound of quartal passages.

The use of perfect fourths melodically is demonstrated in the examples below from "Not Ethiopic" and "Footprints."

This arrangement of one of the all-time great ballads features chords built in fourths.

LAURA

Arranged by NOREEN SAULS

JOHNNY MERCER
DAVID RAKSIN

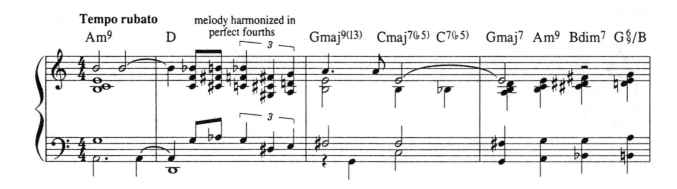

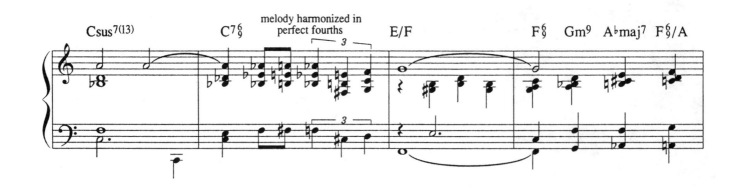

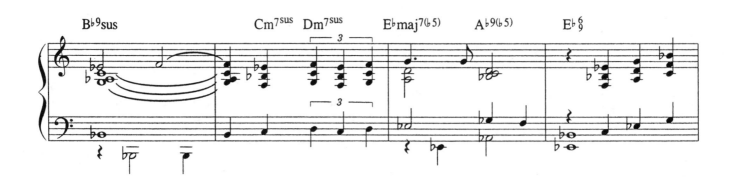

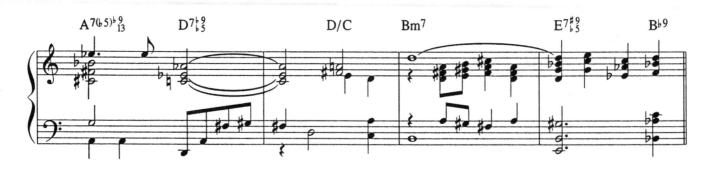

JAZZ PRELUDE
CHILD'S PLAY

STUART ISACOFF

138

JAZZ PRELUDE
RE-BOP

STUART ISACOFF

There's a renewed interest in Mary Lou Williams, who was born May 8,1910, and died in 1981. As an enthusiast who discovered her in the late 1970's, I heard her talk about the eras of jazz: spirituals and blues, Kansas City swing, boogie, bop and modern. And loved her playing.

Father Peter O'Brlen, who has catalogued all of William's work and is the heart and soul of the Mary Lou Williams Foundation, says that "Little Joe " is a portrait. The subject is Joe Glazer, the legendary jazz booking agent and paradigm of a certain style who handled Billie Holiday, Louis Armstrong and many big bands Including Andy Kirk 's Clouds of Joy from Kansas City. Mary Lou arranged and played piano for the band from the late 1920's to 1942. But sometimes she would say that the portrait was of Joe Louis, the fighter. There are five recordings of it: the original, orchestrated for the Clouds of joy; the

1939 piano solo there a 1944 small and version; and two solos from the 70's on Chiaroscuro and Pablo records. The later solos are fuller than the stripped-down, fast-paced boogie woogie of 1939.

Even in the abridged six-chorus solo shown (she originally played eight), this performance shows how strong and agile a player Mary Lou Willams was. "Little Joe" is an endurance test few will pass at her fast, steady tempo.

I've suggested some fingerings, but of course I can't confirm that Mary Lou Williams used them. However, I've tried to use some of the techniques I believe are appropriate. They include same-finger slides from black grace notes to white keys, using the thumb on black keys, and positioning the hand centrally over the keys being played rather than stretching the fourth and fifth fingers.

—Becca Pulliam

LITTLE JOE FROM CHICAGO

(as recorded by Mary Lou Williams)

Transcribed and edited by BECCA PULLIAM

HOAGY CARMICHAEL
SIDNEY ARODIN

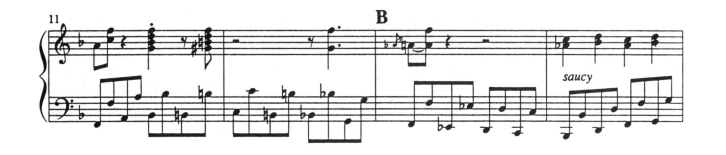

143

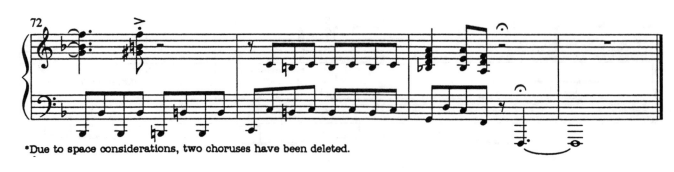

*Due to space considerations, two choruses have been deleted.

144

Mary Lou Williams – Beyond Category

BECCA PULLIAM

Duke Ellington called her "beyond category" because her musicianship was so unlimited. She could play boogie woogie and stride piano with the greats. She was part of the big band era, playing and arranging with equal facility. And she nurtured the next generation of pianists in her own home, making friends of Bud Powell and Thelonious Monk, and allowing the revolutionary new music "bebop" to inhabit her own playing.

There is a unifying principle in Mary Lou Williams' diverse music; it's the blues. The blues is the source of jazz, she said. It's the bedrock of swing, boogie woogie, bop, more modern sounds—all of them bear a close relation to the blues. There's no better way to learn to play jazz than to learn to play the blues, to study how several generations of musicians have expressed their feelings in a single musical setting. The blues has become a universally understood song form in our century. At the beginning of Mary Lou Williams' career, it was new.

For her students, Williams was quick to sketch an example or assignment, often based on the blues. In this issue we have two blues sketches that she gave a lucky student (me!) in 1980. She inscribed "swinging left hand" on the first; on the second, "bop changes."

Both are in F. Both follow the familiar musical progression

But each is sophisticated in a different way. There is more hand motion in the swinging left hand blues, and more harmonic intensity in the bop changes.

To play the swinging left hand, your arm must become a pendulum, anchored at the shoulder. I remember Mary Lou pointing firmly to the center of my forehead and saying that I should have a mental metronome ticking right behind that spot. Even the ninths and tenths, beginning in bar 4, should be played metronomically. Smaller hands will have to "roll" them, bottom to top, to play all the notes.

Play bars 1-5 of each blues to compare the two. In both examples, the momentum intensifies as the bass line descends in bars 1-4. In the swinging version, the descent is faster and steeper. In bars 4-S of the bop version, the chords sound much more colorful. Bar 5 is a moment of temporary rest, or harmonic resolution, in both. At the end of measure 10 and the beginning of measure 11, there's another point of rest, preceding the "turnaround" that prepares the way back to measure 1. In the first blues, Williams resumes the stride style for the turnaround, after four bars of relief from it. In the bop version, she plays four syncopated chords, the voices dropping in steps. I hear much more emotional openness in the bop changes. The major sevenths occurring in many of the voicings have a dissonant edge. The steadily falling inner voices form a countermelody against which you can improvise melodic phrases of your own. Feelings flood the spaces between chordal attacks. The feelings and the music are the blues.

Mary Lou Williams

LULLABY IN RHYTHM

Solo Arrangement by MARY LOU WILLIAMS

BENNY GOODMAN
EDGAR SAMPSON
CLARENCE PROFIT
WALTER HIRSCH

This Mary Lou Williams arrangement is taken from THE GENIUS OF JAZZ GIANTS — Volume 1
distributed by BIG 3/ COLUMBIA PICTURES PUBLICATIONS,P.O. Box 4340, Hialeah, FL 33014

147

Eubie Blake: "Memories of You"

Terry Waldo

Terry Waldo

Terry Waldo transcribed nine Eubie Blake originals for the 1975 folio Sincerely Eubie Blake. *At that time, Blake wrote, "I want to thank Terry Waldo for all his hard work—and for his patience — in deciphering the intricacies of my manuscripts, in listening to records, piano rolls, tapes, even my playing, to I get the most authentic transcriptions possible." A year later, Waldo published the definitive* This Is Ragtime, *in paperback by Da Capo Press. Blake wrote the forward. Waldo transcribed "Memories of You" while he was flying back and forth from Ohio and California to New York, pursuing his various musical projects in the musical theater, film and television.*

Eubie Blake birthday special!

Some years ago, I transcribed a folio of Eubie Blake's numbers for Belwin Mills. It was called *Sincerely Eubie Blake. I* should have included "Memories of You," the song that was actually Blake's theme. Eubie had a wonderful concert arrangement of this song that he often recorded and performed on television.

The first chorus is in the key of F with Eubie's beautiful melody stated in the baritone range, below middle C, and accompanied with grandiose Classical" flourishes. This first *rubato* chorus harks back to the romantic tradition of the nineteenth century— the century of Blake's birth. Eubie really knew how to tug on your heartstrings. But then he pulls a surprise. As "Memories" moves to the key of A♭, it switches with a surprising jolt into a ragtime *tour* de *force*, full of Blake's syncopation tricks.

The foundation of all of Blake's piano music is a strong left hand maintaining the 2/4 ragtime or stride beat. Blake always tapped or stomped his foot in order to maintain this rhythmic foundation. He often played tenths in the left hand. If you can't stretch (Eubie had enormous hands!), a quick roll from the bottom up will do.

The grace notes in the

right hand connected with octave notes (such as bars 38 and 39) are a device Eubie called 'making the notes sing.' It is usually accomplished by striking the black notes and sliding to the successive white notes. There is a similar trick in bar 36, but here the first and fifth fingers slide from the B♭ to the B♮.

There are a couple of neat tricks Blake uses in measures 55-56. He alternates a continuing E♭ grace note in the right hand with a descending chromatic line in the left. The grace notes are first played with a looser, triplet feel in the first bar, but become straight and very short sixteenth notes in the next bar. This is followed two bars later by a dramatic and unexpected silence for over two beats. This is great showbiz by a master musician and entertainer.

The entire piece is accented in a variety of gradations which are difficult to notate. Keep in mind that a conventional accent (<) does not change the duration of the note to which it is applied, while the alternative symbol (∧) cuts the value of the note in half. I would strongly urge listening to Eubie's own rendition on his 1968 Columbia recording *The Eighty-six Years of Eubie Blake (C2S 847).*

Eubie Blake was born February 5, 1883

MEMORIES OF YOU

as played by the composer on The Eighty-six Years of Eubie Blake *(Columbia C2S 847)*

Transcribed by TERRY WALDO

ANDY RAZAF
EUBIE BLAKE

150

151

152

MY MELANCHOLY BABY

Arranged by ANDY LaVERNE

Music by ERNIE BURNETT

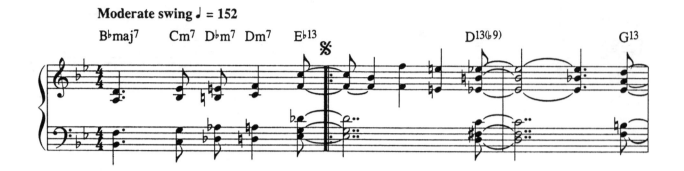

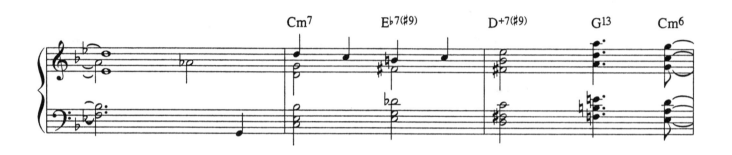

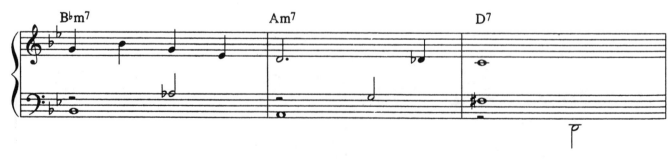

154

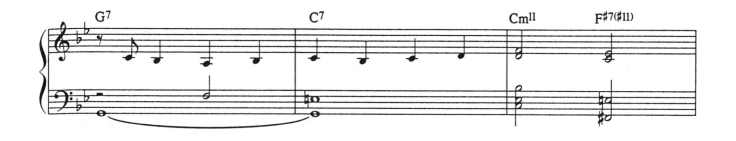

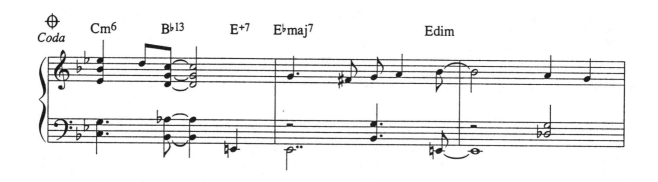

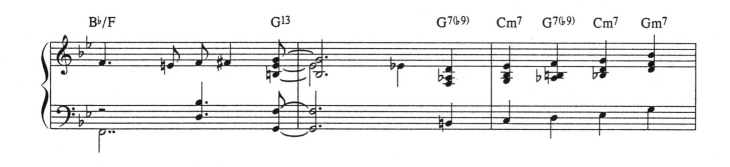

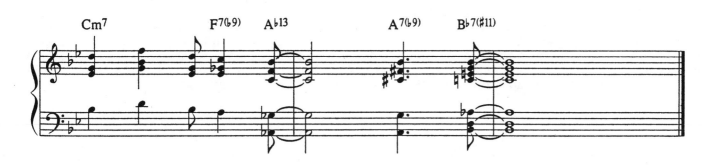

155

Society style piano

Jon Weiss

Jon Weiss is a Manhattanite whose styles range from jazz organ to society style piano.

Society style piano can be thought to date back to the 1800's, the days of Chopin and Liszt, when the pianist performed in a salon setting before a gathering of nobility, wealthy aristocrats, and assorted literati. But back in the 1800's, the music was the focus of such a gathering, and the pianist was sometimes lionized as a Romantic hero. As so often happens, when this tradition migrated to these shores, the outer trappings remained but the culture was lost. Here, the gathering itself (now called a party or affair) became the focus of attention, the musician and his music receded into the background, and the caterer became the hero!

No longer were society ladies swooning and gasping over the impassioned melodies of Chopin or the pyrotechnics of Liszt. Rather they were sipping champagne and sampling exotic hors d'oeuvres while being gently soothed by the popular melodies of the day.

Naturally, musicians being musicians, or the indomitable human spirit being what it is (which is why you can go to some remote village in Mexico or Iran and find the most artfully designed serapes or woolen rugs), the better pianists in the trade were able to develop a rich and sonorous style which still served the function of background or dance music. Some pianists like Eddy Duchin and Carmen Cavallaro developed this style to such an extent that they were able to take it out of the ballroom and onto the airwaves and the concert stage. Peter Nero is a more recent example of someone who has done this.

The emphasis is on the melody

The society style has been influenced by both classical music, particularly from the Romantic period, and whatever trends in jazz were current at the time. Its prominent characteristic is an emphasis on melody, because this is what its audience wants to hear, both on the dance floor or while just lounging. The melody must be clearly stated and played in the correct tempo.

The controlling factor in society music is the tempo. On a typical society job, a tempo is set with an introduction and then a medley of five or six songs is reeled off—each lasting for only one or two choruses. Society tempos tend to fall into certain specific categories. These would include fast two-beat, ballad (really a fox trot), waltz, Viennese waltz (faster), and dixieland. Swing from the 40's and Latin numbers are also played.

Except for the swing and Latin numbers, society tempos differ markedly from those used in jazz. First of all, all of the two-beat numbers and ballads are played in cut time. The up-tempo song "Easy to Love," for example, would normally be played between ♭=76 to ♭=84. A jazz version would be played swing style in 4/4 time. Ballads in society style are usually played in 2/2 between ♭=69 to ♭=76.

Emphasizing the melody led to the development of certain interesting pianistic devices. I have tried to demonstrate some of these in my arrangement of "The Nearness of You." Eddy Duchin developed a style of playing the melody with the right hand in the lower registers of the piano while accompanying it with chords played above it by the left hand (bars 16-20). The most typical device is the so-called triple octave technique whereby the melody is played in octaves or filled-in octaves in the right hand and doubled as the top note of a block chord played an octave or two below it in the left hand.

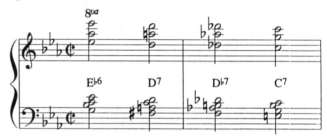

A number of examples of this technique can be found throughout this arrangement (bars 1-4, 6, 30-33). This device is also used to provide a fill in bars 23-24. Carmen Cavallaro created a very smooth chordal style utilizing a variation of this technique. In his playing, the chord with the melody note on top is played in the right hand and the left hand doubles the melody in octaves.

Arpeggios, rapid-fire octaves, and cascading thirds are other devices typical of this style. These are derived from the Romantic piano music with which most society pianists were quite familiar. These devices are most often used as connective material between tones in the melody. Note, for example, the arpeggio in bar 28.

The society style is ideally suited for playing solo piano at restaurants, country clubs, or private parties. It can also be used to provide a *bravura* solo piece as part of a jazz set.

THE NEARNESS OF YOU

in society style

Arranged by JON WEISS

Music by HOAGY CARMICHAEL
Lyric by NED WASHINGTON

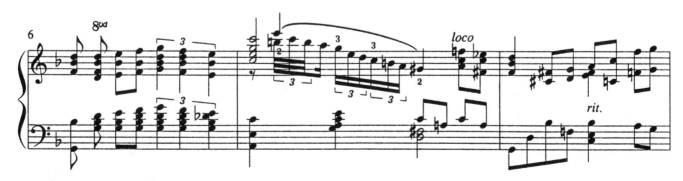

158

159

Mulgrew Miller's voicings for "The Nearness of You"

The busy pianist Mulgrew Miller once gave a clinic in the Bay Area, and he talked about some areas in which he'd been experimenting. To demonstrate, he used "The Nearness of You." Thanks to Mark Levine, we found out about it, and thanks to Mulgrew, we are able to share a moment from his clinic with you.

Miller says, "One of the things I experimented with was playing ballads — to harmonize the melody. This is the basic way you play ballads...

"And then you can reharmonize..."

POLKA DOTS & MOONBEAMS

This reharmonization by Stuart Isacoff shows some of the principles of contrary motion at work.
Arranged by STUART ISACOFF

JOHNNY BURKE
JIMMY VAN HEUSEN

Oscar Hernandez is pianist, arranger, and musical director for artist Ruben Blades and his group Son Del Solar. Hernandez has performed and recorded with artists such as Tito Puente, Celia Cruz, Ray Barretto, Luis Perico Ortiz, Dave Valentin, Linda Ronstadt, Earl Klugh, and others. He is one of the most talented and active pianist/arrangers in the contemporary Latin (salsa) scene.

As much as Latin music has had an influence on all music, and for all its exposure through records, tapes, radio and TV play, there is a scarcity when it comes to printed material. When most people think of or hear Latin music, it always involves a Latin rhythm section (congas, bongos, timbales, maracas, etc.), so a solo piano arrangement is very uncommon. In this case, there's not even recorded material that you can refer to. In my arrangement, there is a four-measure introduction and a four-measure coda. The melody is not changed, and the harmony is the same as the standard "fake book" version except for harmonic substitutions in measures 12-15, 15-16, and 20. What gives the arrangement its character and flavor is the left hand bass which—when combined with the right hand—creates unique and interesting syncopations characteristic of Latin music and rhythms. Have fun! Happy Latin-ing!

OUT OF NOWHERE

Arranged by OSCAR HERNANDEZ

Words by EDWARD HEYMAN
Music by JOHNNY GREEN

Unlocking "Locked Hands" Style

BY ANDY LAVERNE

"**B**lock chords, Red, block chords." Those words, spoken by the late Miles Davis in raspy, barely audible tones, were directed to Red Garland, one of Miles' legendary pianists in the 1950s. The results of those instructions are now classic examples of block chord playing, and can be heard on the Miles Davis recording "Milestones" (Columbia). Red Garland's approach to block chord playing consists of the right hand playing melodic lines in octaves in the upper register of the piano. Between the octaves are chord or scale tones. The left hand chord voicings play the same rhythm as the right hand melody. The result is a full sound, usually with three or four notes in each hand.

This approach differs dramatically from other pianists, including that of another Miles Davis alumnus, Bill Evans. Even though Garland and Evans were contemporaries, their styles were quite different. Bill's block chord playing early on in his career was much like that of the most famous block chord player, George Shearing.

Shearing and Milt Buckner are acknowledged as the originators of the blocked chord concept. Its origins can actually be traced, though, to the big bands of the 1940s — in particular, to the sax section of the Glenn Miller band, which had two altos, two tenors, with either a third tenor or a clarinet added as a top voice. The result was a melody played in octaves, with three inner voices. The term used to describe the top four notes of these voicings is "four way close." Buckner transferred this concept to the keyboard, and Shearing developed and refined it.

The way they distributed the notes on the keyboard was to put the bottom voice in the left hand, the four remaining voices in the right. They used the middle registers of the piano almost exclusively. Bill Evans' depar-

ture from this was in his distribution of notes between the two hands. It is said that he played the top note in his right hand, with the four remaining notes in his left. Although I studied with Bill, I never saw this method of playing block chords up close. However, on a video of Bill playing a version of "Star Eyes," it appears that he is playing with the same note distribution as Shearing uses. In any case, the two hands move in parallel motion, resulting in what has been termed "locked hands." Bill even jokingly referred to himself as the "King of the locked hands." If you hear some of his playing in this style, you might want to take that comment seriously.

> *Bill Evans jokingly referred to himself as the "King of the locked hands."*

Bill's rendition of "Star Eyes" on the video actually inspired me to choose the tune as one of the selections on my recently recorded "Live at Maybeck Hall" solo

164

piano concert (Concord). I decided to do my own interpretation of the locked hands approach, and the following arrangement is taken from my version of "Star Eyes" for this recording. On the recording, however, I freely interpreted the rhythm, playing in a rubato manner, and using arpeggiation within the confines of the block chords.

The big question in locked hands playing is how to fill in those octaves. Depending on what you're playing, and at what tempo it's being played, it is not always necessary to fill in the octaves. The illusion of five notes can be conveyed, if not articulated. There are, however, some solid methods to use when five notes are desired, thus eliminating the guess work. The most common method of "four way close," with a double melody, is alternating 6th chords (or 7th chords), and diminished chords. In reality, this can be broken down into alternating I chords and V chords, because diminished chords are actually incomplete dominant seventh chords.

The following examples show how to voice block chords for major, minor, and dominant seventh chords. Play through these, using either the Shearing or the Evans method, and see which feels more natural to you. As with all theoretical information, transpositions to all other tonal centers will serve you well. After you check out these voicings, play the arrangement of "Star Eyes," and see if you can identify the methods used. Keep in mind this is but one approach to block chords, a challenging and rewarding concept with endless possibilities and applications. ■

Locked Hands Practice Drill

165

STAR EYES

Arranged by ANDY LaVERNE

DON RAYE
GENE de PAUL

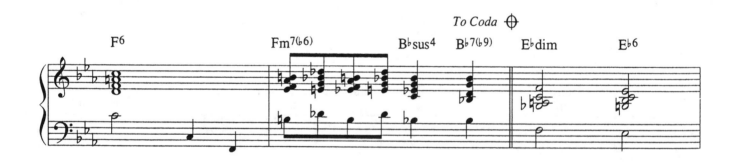

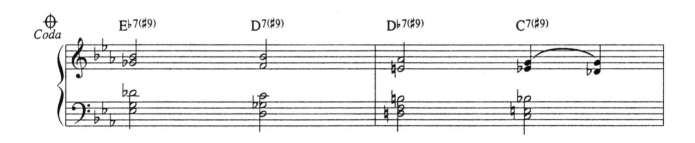

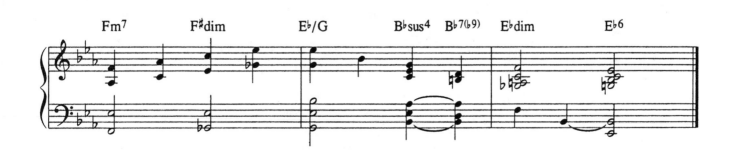

167

STAR EYES

Arranged by MARK LEVINE

DON RAYE
GENE de PAUL

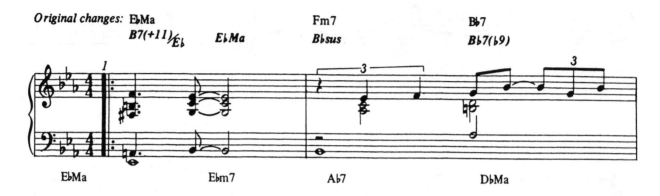

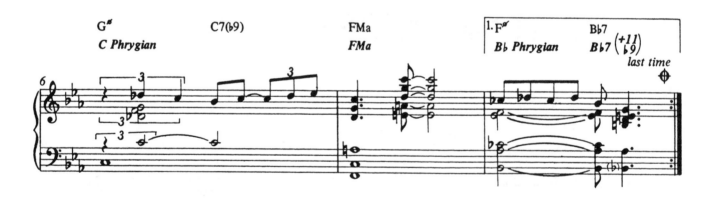

$^{\varnothing}$ means half diminished, i.e., m7(b5).

"alt" means altered, i.e., the ninth may be raised and/or lowered, the eleventh raised, and the thirteenth lowered. Another common chord symbol for D7alt is D7$\left(\begin{smallmatrix}+5\\b5\\+9\\b9\end{smallmatrix}\right)$. The appropriate altered scale would be D—Eb—F—F#—Ab—Bb—C—D.

Sus and Phrygian chords
by Mark Levine

Some of the musicians with whom Mark Levine has recorded are Cal Tjader and Carmen McRae, Joe Henderson, and Poncho Sanchez. His own album, Smiley and Me, is on Concord Jazz. Mark teaches jazz piano at Sonoma State University and lives and works in the San Francisco Bay area.
This is an excerpt from The Jazz Piano Book by Mark Levine, by Sher Music.

Although Duke Ellington was playing them in the 1930's, **sus** chords have been an everyday sound in jazz only since the 1960's. The simplest voicing — whether you're playing a standard or Herbie Hancock's "Maiden Voyage" — is to play the root with your left hand while playing a major triad a whole step below the root with your right hand, as in figure 1.

Because G is the root of this sus chord, the triad in your right hand would be F major, a whole step below G. Note that the triad is in second inversion, meaning that the fifth of the triad (C) is on the bottom, instead of the root (F). Triads often sound stronger inverted than in root position, especially so when in second inversion. The **Gsus** chord resolves smoothly to a **CMa7**.

The "sus" refers to the suspended fourth of the chord, in this case the note C. In traditional harmony, this note usually resolves downward a half step, the sus chord becoming a dominant seventh chord (figure 2). In modern music, this note often doesn't resolve, which gives sus chords their "floating" quality.

You might see this same **Gsus** chord notated as **G7sus4, Gsus4, F/G,** or **Dm7/G. F/G** describes exactly what's happening in figure 1: an F triad in the right hand over the note G in the left hand. **Dm7/G** describes the *function* of the sus chord, because a sus chord is like a II-V progression contained in one chord. The **II-V** progression in the key of C is **Dm7-G7**. In figure 3, your right hand plays a common **Dm7** left hand voicing over a G root, combining **Dm7** and **G7** into a single chord — **Dm7/G,** or **Gsus.**

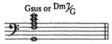

Two songs recorded in the 1960's did a lot to popularize sus chords among jazz musicians: John Coltrane's "Naima"[1] and Herbie Hancock's "Maiden Voyage."[2] "Maiden Voyage" consists entirely of sus chords, which made it a revolutionary tune for its time. Hancock's vamp on the first two bars is shown in figure 4. The **Dsus** chord is voiced with a C triad a whole step down from the root, D. One note in the triad has been doubled, and the fifth has been added in the left hand to give the chord more "bottom."

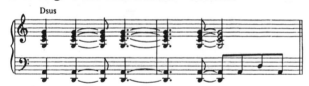

A persistent misconception about sus chords is that the fourth takes the place of the third. Jazz pianists, however, often voice the third with a sus chord, as you can see in the examples in the next figure. Note that in the first five voicings shown, the third is above the fourth. You could play the fourth above the third, as in the last voicing, but the result would be a much more dissonant chord. In a tune like "Maiden Voyage," where each sus chord lasts for four bars, you have a lot more freedom to use dissonance. Let your taste be your guide.

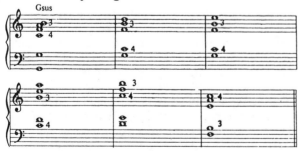

Phrygian chords

A Phrygian chord is a dominant seventh chord with the thirteenth in the bass instead of the root. The next figure shows a G7 voicing with the root in the bass and the same G7 voicing with its thirteenth, E, in the bass. You might

see a Phrygian chord notated as **G7/E, Esusb9,**or **E Phryg** — since there is no single commonly accepted chord symbol for a Phrygian chord.

If you know the major modes, you know that Phrygian is the third mode of the major scale, and that E Phrygian is derived from the third note of the C major scale. The alternate chord symbol **G7/E** gives a clue to what's happening here. Instead of playing G in the bass, you substitute E, the Phrygian note in the key of C. Notice how smoothly it resolves to the **AMa** chord. Even though **G7** is a V chord in the key of C, the **V-I** relationship here is between **E** and **A.**

A beautiful example of Phrygian harmony is the **Eb Phrygian** chord in the intro and the next-to-last chord on the bridge of John Coltrane's "After The Rain" on *Impressions* (MCA-5887).

You can use sus and Phrygian chords effectively to reharmonize standard tunes, as in the accompanying arrangement of "Star Eyes." The original chords are shown above the reharmonized chord symbols. Whenever a sus or Phrygian chord appears, it takes the place of a II or V chord, or substitutes for the entire II-V progression.

The melody has been changed in bar 4 to accommodate the **Ab Phrygian** chord. There are some other goodies here, too. In particular, note the Duke Ellington-like chords in bars 1 and 3, the McCoy Tyner-like fourth chords in bars 10 and 14, and the Kenny Barron style minor seventh voicing in bar 16. The very last chord is a sus chord in a completely different key. This touch gives an ethereal quality to the ending.

Try your hand at reharmonizing tunes using sus and Phrygian chords. I would suggest "I Didn't Know What Time It Was," "Yesterdays," "Stella By Starlight," and "What Is This Thing Called Love." ●

---

[1] John Coltrane, *Giant Steps*, Atlantic SD-1311.
[2] Herbie Hancock, *Maiden Voyage*, Blue Note 84195.

Fred Hersch's album, "Red Square Blue," on the Angel label, features this evocative jazz arrangement of a Prelude by Russian composer Alexander Scriabin. "I like the fact that the rhythm of the piece is really coming from the second beat and that most of the phrases continue across the barline, something I try to do whenever I improvise in 3/4 time," reports Fred. "The fun of playing this piece as an improvisor is to allow the written material to really affect your solos, so that it all becomes seamlessly integrated into one fabric."

PRELUDE

FRED HERSCH
ALEXANDER SCRIABIN

D.S. 𝄋 al Coda ⊕

⊕ Coda

rit.

173

PRELUDE IN E MAJOR
NO. 2

ROLAND P. HANNA
(1932-   )

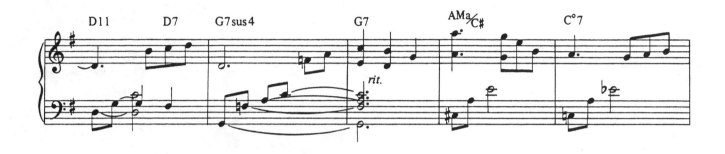

Stuart Isacoff studied with Sir Roland Hanna in the 1970's. We asked him to write a postscript for the Prelude in E Major, No. 2.

Roland Hanna's style is one of a kind, because of the unusual combination of influences one finds in his music. There is his love of Wagner and Chopin, for instance, which lends his approach a romantic chromaticism and a concern with voice leading more reminiscent of a classical tradition than a jazz one (how often do we hear jazz pianists employing simple parallel motion to move from one overused dominant voicing to another?). That regard for romanticism is an important element in understanding this jazz master. While his technical command would enable him to play virtually anything and everything on the piano, he has never abandoned those traditions and values — European, African, and American — that represent to him the highest levels of musical craftsmanship, and he has little patience for styles that neglect lyricism or structure. (Note, for Romantic flavoring, his use of the b9 and b6 as melody notes on ''strong'' beats.) Sir Roland also creates a somewhat symphonic

sound by doubling voices (see measure 9) and by using full but triadic harmonies at times (note the right hand chord in measure 49).

Another element of his sound can be seen in measure 15. Hanna often uses quartel harmonies, but he likes them strong and full, and therefore plays them in a way different from the norm. Many contemporary players would use the right hand harmony in the first chord of measure 15 with just the two bottom notes of the left hand chord, to produce a sound built on ''fourths.'' But here, the insertion of the G# in the left hand produces a stack of open fifths on the bottom of the harmony, and lends it a different, richer sound. The fullness of Roland Hanna's harmonies is one of his trademarks, and the way he moves from one to another is the real story of his style.

Round Midnight is available by mail from Town Crier Recordings, Department PS, 205 West 89th Street, New York, NY 10024. Send $13.98 for the CD, $9.98 for a cassette tape. Add $2 shipping and handling. Later in the year, Hanna plans to publish more transcriptions from the recording. We'll let you know when they become available. ●

Duke Ellington: Piano Player

JED DISTLER

Nearly twenty years after his death, Duke Ellington's stature as one of this century's creative giants looms larger than ever. Most of his recordings are available now more than ever before. Hardly a month goes by without a re-release of some long out-of-print gem or previously unknown live dance date. Jazz musicians and cabaret singers keep his pop tunes alive, while ambitious large scale works are resurrected by jazz repertory ensembles and choreographers. Several Ellington piano rarities not generally available to the public in sheet music form are included in this issue.

Although the orchestra that bore his name was Duke Ellington's "real" instrument, he always referred to himself as "the piano player in the band." The piano was a springboard for his musical ideas, and an instrument was always provided for him in his hotel room so he could compose on the road. His rich harmonic sense and unique chord voicings stem directly from his piano playing.

Born on April 29,1899 in Washington, D.C., Edward Kennedy Ellington had his first piano lessons When he was seven. His teacher's name was, of all things, Mrs. Clinkscales. Like most kids, his struggles with Czerny exercises were pure torture and he soon quit. But his interest in music rekindled as a teenager and he began playing professionally. Ellington was impressed with the local stride "ticklers," mainly for the flashy left hand technique, but also, as he admitted, for their reputation as ladies men. Years later, as the recipient of countless testimonials and award ceremonies in his honor, Duke would always oblige his hosts with a piano solo. He'd invariably dedicate it to the most beautiful woman in the room, usually the wife of an important dignitary or head of state.

Ellington made light of his keyboard prowess, preferring instead to shower accolades on, well, just about everyone else. No jazz artist could have had a more supportive colleague. He encouraged Oscar Peterson to embark on a solo recital career. At the same time, he championed Thelonious Monk years before the critics caught on (Monk's piano style in fact borrowed a lot from Duke's own). Some of Ellington's young piano proteges included such diverse talents as Abdullah Inbrahim and Claude Bolling. Closest to his heart, though, were his youthful mentors, stride masters James P. Johnson and Willie "The Lion" Smith.

> *Duke's conception of a tune was never fixed, no matter how many times he may have played it.*

Throughout his long career Ellington's piano playing was, and still is, underrated. Although solos on earlier records are often technically and rhythmically unsettled, there are a few examples of thrilling stride playing. The 1932 "Lots O' Notes" is a notable example. But his was not a soloists temperament. He developed instead into a peerless orchestral pianist, with an instantly recognizable touch. Helped by his razor sharp timbre, he could energize the orchestra, sometimes just by a few perfectly place notes, as in "C Jam Blues" or "Perdido."

Above all there are Duke's inimitable introductions, particu-

larly on late '30s, and early '40s records. What is so remarkable about them is that Ellington was able, within a few seconds, with fantastic harmonic invention, to place the sound world and the emotional essence of the whole work. His most copied introductions are for "Satin Doll" and "Take The A Train." Often in live performance Ellington would expand these intros, which eventu-

Duke in the solo spotlight.

ally evolved into new pieces. "Kinda Dukish" was originally the introduction to the band's flagwaving opener, "Rocking In Rhythm." One marvels at the unexpected ways in which Duke explores all the registers of the keyboard, unlike many of the bop pianists who rarely traveled beyond a three-octave compass.

And what is more recognizably Duke than the trademark downward arpeggios, so endearingly slapdash and border-line cocktail lounge? Listen to his wacky 1945 trio version of the traditional "Frankie and Johnny" to hear how he could play them pretty cleanly when he chose.

Ellington recorded extensively as soloist with rhythm section and with small groups, starting in the early '50s. All those recordings are currently available on CD. The BMG compilation, "Solos, Duets and Trios," covers most of the RCA piano material from 1932-1966, all the Ellington/Jimmy Blanton duets from 1940 and the above mentioned "Lots O' Fingers" and "Frankie and Johnny." A unique two-piano session with his right hand man, Billy Strayhorn, is also available ("Great Times" on Fantasy), but it is pitched a half-tone sharp (as was the original 10 inch LP).

It's instructive to hear how Duke's conception of a tune was never fixed, no matter how many hundreds of times he may have played it. Compare the 1941 solo version, both takes, of *"Solitude"* with those from the later Charles Mingus/Max Roach trio session. The earlier ones are pensive but elegant, while the later ones are more brooding and harmonically complex.

What all Duke Ellington's piano recordings have in common is a sense of discovery and spontaneous exploration, as well as the sheer joy in playing with others in an intimate setting. It's difficult to think of another jazz pianist who got a bigger kick out of playing.

Jazz lovers know that Duke Ellington wrote many, many hundreds of works for small groups, full bands, and even orchestra. But Duke also composed many pieces for solo piano, many of which he never recorded or published. "When Duke was in town," says Sacramento jazz trumpeter Joe Ingram, "he used to come by to sit in with our band. On the intermissions he'd stay at the piano and play the loveliest pieces. 'What's that?' I'd ask him, and he'd say, 'Oh, just a little something I made up.' No one had ever heard them—or would ever hear them again."

One piece that Duke did record (in 1953, with bassist Wendell Marshall) is his rhapsodic "Reflections In D" (reissued on the Capital Jazz CD "Duke Ellington, Piano Reflections"), on which this transcription is based. The entire piece is played very freely, out of tempo; the time values in such a performance are, therefore, highly subjective. And Duke changes the music quite a bit on each repeat. I recommend listening to Duke's recording to get the composition's true feeling. —*Andrew Fielding*

REFLECTIONS IN D

Transcribed by ANDREW FIELDING

DUKE ELLINGTON

181

I wrote this half-improvised chorus of "Solitude" keeping in mind Ellington's early piano style and his stride background. The characteristics are the stride bass as well as the backbeat accompaniment found in the bridge. Backbeats are displacements of the regular motion of a stride left hand, and they were widely used by Ellington's early role models such as James P. Johnson and

Willie "the Lion" Smith. Here and there I also took some liberties with the original chord changes of this tune, as you can see in bars 5-4 and 11-12, where I used some chromatically descending chords in place of the original E♭Ma7. The harmonic solution featured in bar 31 is possibly a bit odd, but it sounds good to me, so I used it!
- Riccardo Scivales

SOLITUDE

Arranged by RICCARDO SCIVALES

IRVING MILLS, EDDIE DeLANGE
& DUKE ELLINGTON

This arrangement is based on George Gershwin's treatment of "My Man's Gone Now," found earlier in this collection.

─SOMETIMES I FEEL LIKE A─
MOTHERLESS CHILD

Arranged by NOREEN SAULS

SPIRITUAL

185

Carmen Cavallaro — Piano "Poet"

By Noreen Sauls

Carmen Cavallaro

I have always been a fan of old biographical movies about musicians. "The Eddy Duchin Story," with it's wonderfully executed musical score is one of them. It was a great surprise for me to learn, while researching this article, that the "behind the scenes" pianist for this soundtrack was actually Carmen Cavallaro (1913-1989).

Known as the "Poet of the Piano," Carmen was born in New York City. He was a child prodigy, and during his early teens he began playing popular music with local club orchestras on weekends. Soon, he had a regular place in Al Kavelin's orchestra. Later, he also performed with band led by Rudy Vallee, Enric Madriguera and Abe Lyman.

The year 1941 brought about two major events: the formation of Carmen's own orchestra and an offer from Decca Records to cut an album. The success of that album gained tremendous popularity for him. More recordings followed, and his orchestra was in constant demand for hotel, theater, nightclub and radio engagements around the country; he also appeared in several musical films.

Carmen's style was lyrical, liquid, somewhat ornate, and expertly executed with a well-developed technique. Some people may think of it as a "corny" or "society" type of playing, but it represents a chapter in the history of jazz piano that should not be overlooked. Among the many pianists who played in this genre, Carmen was one of the truly talented. The clearly stated melodies are perfectly balanced with fills, runs, arpeggios and octaves.

Two selections arranged by Carmen Cavallaro are featured in this collection. We'll examine some of his ideas, so you can incorporate them into your own approach.

"So Rare" begins with contrapuntal, contrary motion between the two hands. This is repeated in each A section of the tune. Many of the runs Carmen used are easier than they sound — they utilize familiar scales and arpeggios. For instance, in measure 5, the right hand plays an A Flat pentatonic scale (Ab, Bb, C, Eb, F), ending with some chromaticism into measure 6. Likewise, measure 11 consists of a C6 run (ascending), and a C major scale (descending) — split between the hands.

Measures 12 and 13 are based on a II-V-I progression in A Flat. The right hand of measure 12 is based on the A Flat major scale, while measure 13 is a repeat of measure 5.

In measure 15, beats 3 and 4 center around stepwise descending chords voiced in fifths (FMaj.7, Em7, Dm7, Cmaj.7). This is a good progression to learn in all keys. In measure 19, the left hand arpeggio figures are E Flat (ascending) and D Flat (descending). See what other devices you can find in this song. One of Carmen's "signatures" appears in the final three measures, where unison octaves are used. This, and upper register embellishments, allow the piano to be heard easily over an orchestra.

In "You Stepped Out Of A Dream," the melodic filler in measures 1 and 3 consist of "bell" tones built from C6-9 and D Flat 6-9, respectively.

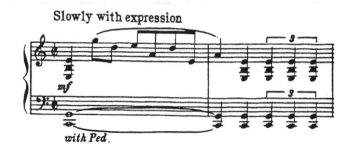

Measures 4 to 7 make up a II-V-I progression in A Flat. The left hand is quite active, using notes almost exclusively from the A Flat major scale.

186

Notes from the F pentatonic scale can be found in the left hand arpeggio of measures 11 and 12. This leads to a D7 chord in measure 13. The 32nd-note ascending run is simply one pattern played in three consecutive octaves. This occurs again, in measure 29, on a descending Dm11 pattern, and in measure 23, beginning with the right hand middle C. The chord here is a G Flat dominant 7th with a flat 5.

all keys. The left hand here focuses primarily on Root-5th-10th voicings.

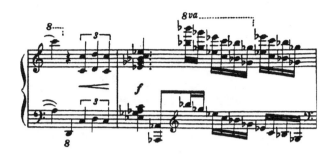

Measures 15 and 16 feature unison octaves, in similar fashion to the ending of "So Rare." From measure 27 to the end, he uses a progression well worth practicing in

The right hand "bell" tones of measures 31 and 32 are reminiscent of measures 1 and 3, bringing the arrangement full cricle. The final three measures use notes from a C6-9 chord, creating a very open sound.

After playing the arrangements, do a complete harmonic analysis of each one, so you can discover the origin of all the embellishments. Pick out your favorite ones, develop your own variations on them, and try applying them to other tunes.

If you've never hear Carmen Cavallaro play, pick up one of his recordings — *The Good Music Record Company presents The Very Best Of Carmen Cavallaro* is a good choice — or rent "The Eddy Duchin Story" video. ■

SO RARE

Arranged by CARMEN CAVALLARO

Words by JACK SHARPE
Music by JERRY HERST

189

YOU STEPPED OUT OF A DREAM

Arranged by CARMEN CAVALLARO

Words by GUS KAHN
Music by NACIO HERB BROWN

Also see the article appearing after "So Rare" in this book.

SPRING IS HERE

Arranged by BILL CHARLAP

Music by RICHARD ROGERS
Words by LORENZ HART

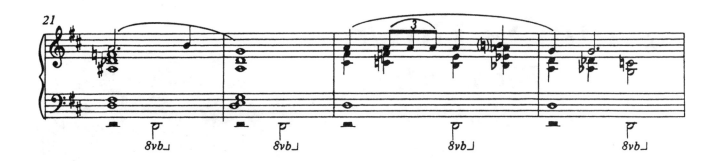

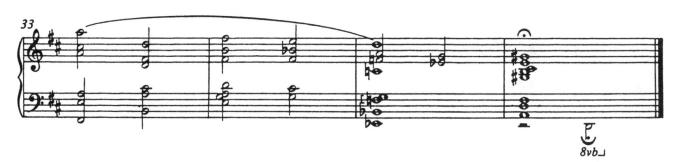

Bill Charlap is a free-lance pianist in the New York area whose performance credits include piano duos with Dick Hyman and playing piano in Gerry Mulligan's quartet and big band. Charlap is also a student of classical pianist Eleanor Hancock. Now, a note from Bill:

"This arrangement is basically just a sketch of how I might play 'Spring Is Here' in a solo piano context. When I improvise on an arrangement such as this one, I tend to focus more on pianistic types of embellishments (such as arpeggiated patterns and other coloristic devices) than linear improvisation. The arrangement can be played exactly as written, but I encourage adding to or deleting from any part of it to suit your personal taste. For three other possibilities, listen to Bill Evans' *Portrait in Jazz*, Richie Beirach's *Elegy for Bill Evans*, or Kenny Barron's *Landscape* album. I hope you enjoy this arrangement of 'Spring Is Here.' "

Bill Charlap

Thumbs Down
Fat Sounds For Small Hands

BY PRESTON KEYS

Getting a full sound on the piano with small hands can be an awesome task. If your hands are unable to reach all the major tenths with ease, it is essential that you develop other techniques in order to play tunes with as full a sound as possible. Here is just one.

It would be difficult if not impossible to play the notes of the following chord simultaneously in the form in which it is notated.

The following version which uses the left thumb to play the top two notes in the left-hand part is considerably easier because there is not such an awkward right-hand part.

To give some examples of how easy it is to use this technique, I have written out various chords, each with two versions. The first version of each chord is written without the use of the thumb; the second version includes the thumb on two adjacent notes.

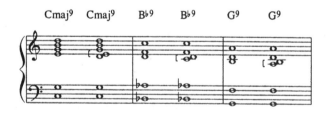

Two adjacent black notes as well as two adjacent white notes can be played at the same time with the thumb.

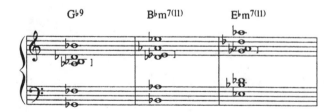

Even larger-sounding chords than those written above can be played, provided that one can reach a white-to-white tenth, or any minor tenth in the bass.

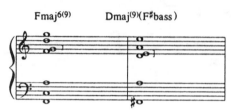

Since these chords really sound big, they can be used when emphasis is needed. The next example illustrates a short melody which begins with one of these "reinforced" chords.

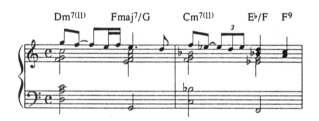

Finally, here is a demonstration of how left-hand chords that employ seconds played with the thumb can provide a "cushion" when improvising with the right hand.

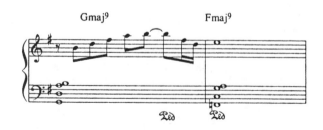

Preston Keys is at work on a book that details various ways that pianists with small hands can produce "fat" sounds.

194

Here is an arrangement based on the use of thumbs for striking more than one note at a time, as outlined in the article preceding this piece of music. (The brackets indicate the use of one finger to strike two notes.) Experiment with the approach — you may find you can make the voicings used here even thicker, with a little effort.

SWEET & LOVELY

Arranged by PRESTON KEYS

GUS ARNHEIM
HARRY TOBIAS
JULES LEMARE

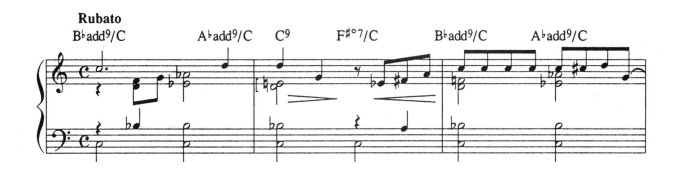

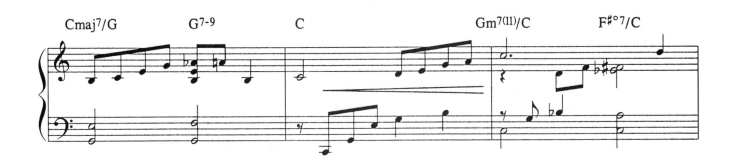

195

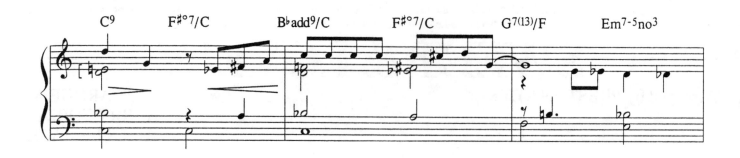

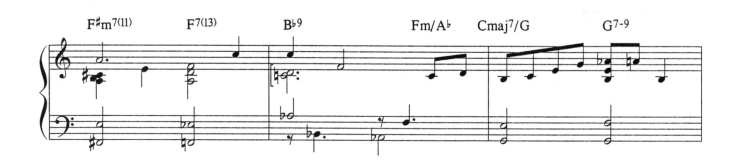

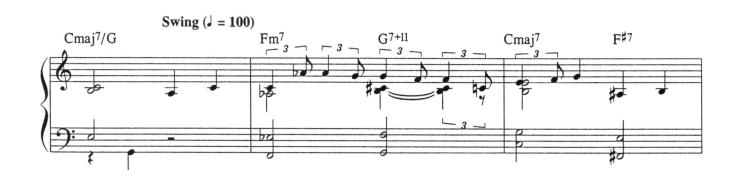

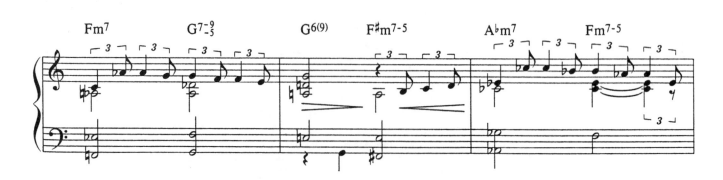

196

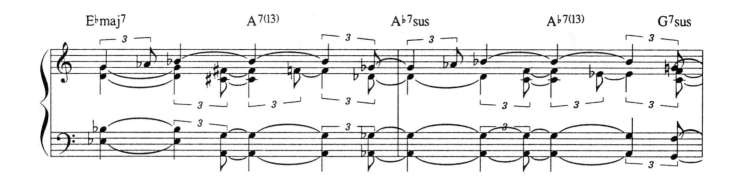

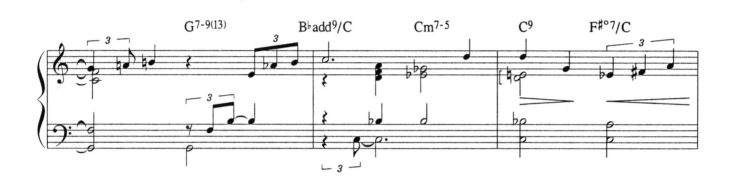

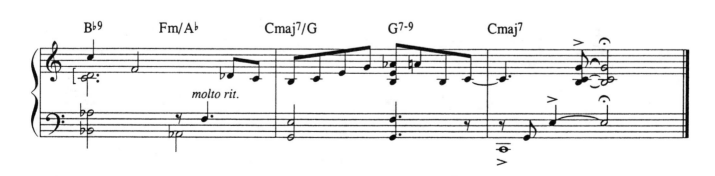

Carmen Cavallaro's approach is a lesson in "Society Style" piano playing.

TAKING A CHANCE ON LOVE

Arranged by CARMEN CAVALLARO

JOHN LATOUCHE
TED FETTER
VERNON DUKE

For a down-home blues with out a hint of boogie, try this two-fisted piece by Dave Brubeck from his Peanuts television special, now available in the collection "Quiet As The Moon" (CPP/Belwin).

TRAV'LIN' BLUES

DAVE BRUBECK

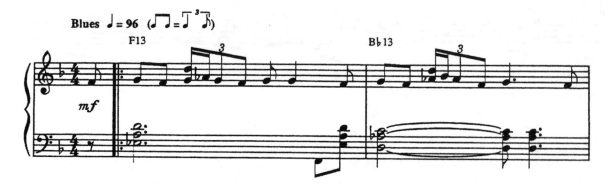

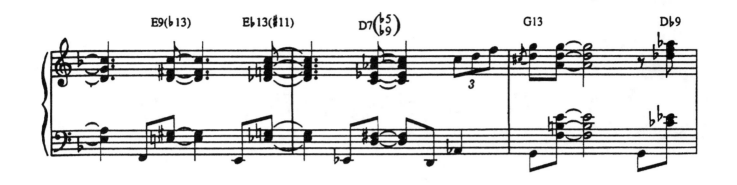

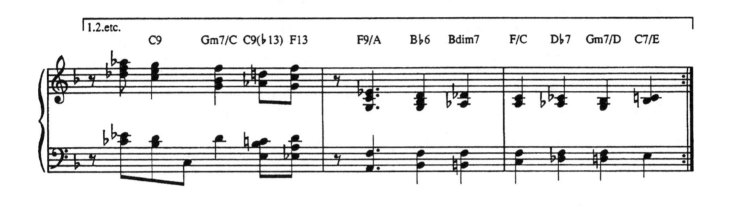

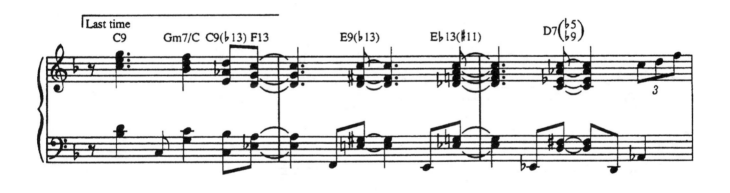

Reharmonizing "Stella by Starlight"

by Andy LaVerne

Last month, we examined some of the techniques to use in the process of reharmonization. This month, I present my reharmonized arrangement of "Stella by Starlight" for you to study. Ideally, I'd like you to play through the piece and see how many of the techniques are being put to use. There are, however, some thoughts and decisions behind this version of "Stella" that no amount of analysis can reveal.

One is my motivation for reharmonizing such a familiar standard. Certainly, the original harmonies need no *improvement*. For years, people — myself included — have been listening to and playing this tune, and deriving great satisfaction from it. But it is in the jazz tradition to sculpt the material to personalize a sound or style.

Recently, I played a duo gig with guitarist John Abercrombie. Even though we are both composers, we focused mostly on standard tunes. I enjoyed the entire playing experience, and the greatest rush of pleasure came from reharmonizing another familiar standard, "All the Things You Are." This gave me the impetus to expand my repertoire of reharmonized standards. "Stella" immediately came to mind.

The approach I use here is a new one for me.

My idea is to play the standard melody and completely change the harmonic structure under it. It's almost as if I pretend that I am composing anew. The thing I want to keep in mind is to make this a "benign" reharmonization — in other words, different chords, different functions, but overall a similar feeling. My objectives are to give myself a new and challenging set of chord changes and give the listener some pleasant surprises as a result.

It is in the jazz tradition to sculpt the material to a personal style.

At this point, I am still so intrigued with the new chords that just playing the melody for several choruses while shifting some voicings and inner voice movements seems to preclude melodic improvisation. But an alternative form would be to alternate the solo choruses between the standard changes and these new ones. Is this a precursor to composition? Ponder that question, and enjoy the music on pages 14-15! ●

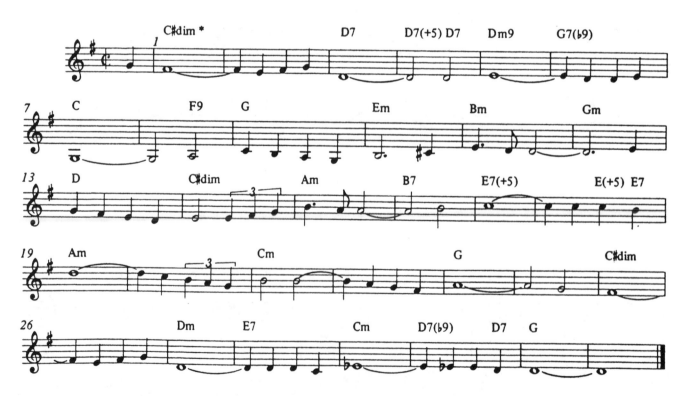

* *Original chord symbols and melody in key of G.*
Melody is in a vocalist's range. The piano arrangement shows it one octave higher.

STELLA BY STARLIGHT

Arranged by ANDY LaVERNE

VICTOR YOUNG
NED WASHINGTON

* ∅7 = m7(♭5)

Bill Evans reharmonization

Mulgrew Miller's arrangement of "Warm Valley"

Nearly fifty years after he wrote it, Duke Ellington's "Warm Valley" has never been published as a piano arrangement until now. The Ellington Orchestra recorded the ballad in 1940 with the romantic alto saxophone of Johnny Hodges playing the lead. (The Smithsonian Collection album Duke Ellington 1940 (R013) has two takes of "Warm Valley.") The melody has been compared to "Sweet and Lovely" and the bridge (**B** section) has been compared to the **B** section of Billy Strayhorn's "Chelsea Bridge."

Mulgrew Miller spent three years (1977-80) as the pianist with the Duke Ellington Orchestra. That's where he learned "Warm Valley," and he recorded it on his 1985 album Keys to the City (Landmark LLP1507). We asked him to talk about the features of his solo piano arrangement.

One striking feature is Miller's occasional fast, brilliant right hand runs between melodic phrases. Miller says it's no accident that he uses colorful runs in "Warm Valley" because playing Ellington's music heightened his awareness of chromatic harmony. He chooses a run to "address the color in the chord," whether it be a b9 or +9, +11, b13 or whatever.

Look at the F# minor scale at the end of the introduction. The chord in that bar is an F7.

The notes in the F# minor run create an F7 (b9, +9, b13) chord when played in the voicing above.

Look at the other run, in bar 30. This is also a six-note minor scale on the key of B. Miller

---

It's no accident that Miller uses colorful runs in "Warm Valley" because playing Ellington's music heightened his awareness of chromatic harmony.

---

puts a little "hook" at the top before he begins descending through the keys. The scale creates a Bb7 (b9, +9, b13) chord, the dominant (V) chord of Eb. And Eb is the chord of resolution in bar 31.

Miller strikes the Eb in octaves emphatically on the first beat of the bar. He uses an athletic metaphor to describe the action, saying his left hand "intercepts" his right hand here. "My left hand is waiting to intercept my right, resolving the harmony by playing the next chord."

Left hand techniques

It should be very helpful to practice this arrangement hands alone and to pay undivided attention to your left hand. You'll find allusions to stride piano in bars 11-12. (Miller is an excep-

tional stride pianist.) He strikes a pedal fifth in bar 15, then lifts his left hand to a higher register to join the right in harmonizing the melody. Besides arpeggiated chords (broken chords) using the root, fifth and tenth (bars 6, 14 and 27, for example), he also introduces "walking tenths" in bar 34.

The left hand counter-melodies exquisitely balance the melodic phrases in the right hand, especially in the beginnings of the phrases at each **A** section. Here are the first two.

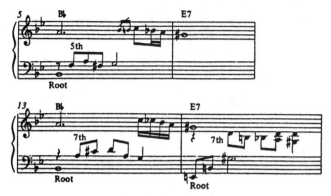

Notice how the melody flows conversationally. When the left hand "speaks," the right hand is quiet. The original melody is part of the composition, but where does the counter-melody come from? Miller points out that it often begins on the fifth or the seventh of the chord. The contours of the melody and counter-melody are similar, rising then falling, in an arc.

As you put your hands together, you'll be able to appreciate the complex chord voicings such as the E7/D7 in bar 8. Miller leaves an octave of musical space between his hands here. The effect is to lift the color tones out of the lower register chord and to allow these tones to carry beautifully from the higher register of the piano.

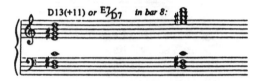

More runs

Mulgrew Miller's fast fingers allow him to play long runs in a split second. He says he doesn't think about the rhythmic subdivisions of the beat so much as he simply plays the run until it's time to move on to the next chord.

We asked Miller for ideas for other runs and he easily supplied these:

1. In bar 7, on beat 4, approaching the D7 in bar 8, play a descending six-tone scale that outlines an Eb13 (+11) chord. He points out that it's also a Bb minor scale with a major seventh.

2. In bar 22, on beats 3-4, over the C#7, play an FMa7 (+5) arpeggio Notice the fingering!

3. In bar 28, on beats 3-4, play a diminished scale in parallel thirds.
The scale gives a C7 (b9, +9, +11) sound to the F7(+5).●

Duke Ellington's introduction to "Warm Valley" from the 1940 recording.

WARM VALLEY

Arranged by MULGREW MILLER
Transcribed by RON ROULLIER

DUKE ELLINGTON
(1899-1974)

WHEN I GROW TOO OLD TO DREAM

Arranged by PRESTON KEYS

OSCAR HAMMMERSTEIN II
SIGMUND ROMBERG

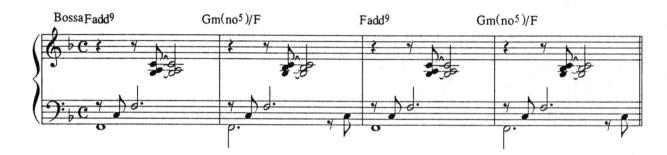

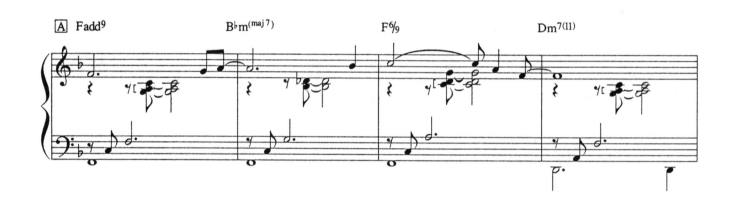

211

WHEN I GROW TOO OLD TO DREAM

as recorded on Hampton Hawes at the Piano (Contemporary S7637)

Transcribed by NOREEN SAULS

OSCAR HAMMMERSTEIN II
SIGMUND ROMBERG

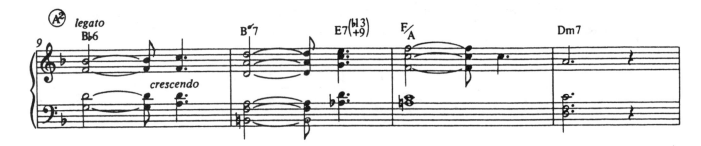

Last chorus of the piano solo

* Chord symbols shown are the basic changes for the tune.

Simplicity, gospel, the blues, and bebop: the style of Hampton Hawes

by Noreen Sauls

Noreen Sauls teaches at William Paterson College and the University of Bridgeport, and plays around and about New York, often with her husband, bassist Earl Sauls.

Noreen Sauls

I'll never forget the first time I heard a Hampton Hawes recording. My husband turned me on to him in 1979 (two years after the pianist's death), and I have loved Hawes' playing ever since.

Creating this transcription fulfills one of my longtime musical fantasies. I have wanted to discover what makes Hampton's piano style instantly recognizable. Reading his autobiography, *Raise Up Off Me* (written with Don Asher), also enlightened me about his upbringing, personal difficulties, and the musical influences that shaped his style.

His performance of "When I Grow Too Old to Dream" is from the posthumously released trio album *Hampton Hawes at the Piano* with bassist Ray Brown and drummer Shelly Manne (Contemporary Records S7657). This record is one of my personal favorites and one of Hampton's best. If you don't own this album, you're missing some great music.

While transcribing, I got carried away and wrote down the whole tune. But we have limited space, so only the "in-head" and the third (and final) piano chorus are presented here.

He plays the melody on the in-head simply, with a bluesy feel and two- and three-note left hand chords possessing the gospel quality so evident in Hamp's music. His father was a Presbyterian minister, and the church music with which he grew up played an important part in his musical development.

Notice the rhythmic and harmonic sparseness of the left hand in both choruses of the transcription. Very often, only one or two notes are used. Look at bars 17-20 in the impro-

vised chorus. The major thirds and perfect fourths in the left hand balance the much more active right hand. Don't overlook this point when you play. We pianists are often so concerned with intricate (sometimes thick) voicings, altered chords, and substitutions that we lose sight of the many simple things that can enhance our music.

Also uncomplicated, but effective, are the first three measures of the solo. The right hand consists mainly of F and D, and the left hand is an inverted F triad. But the rhythmic figures generate the tension and momentum that leads into the explosion of chords in bar 4.

Hampton's trademark bluesy right hand licks are best illustrated in bars 7-8 and 28-30 of the improvised solo. These patterns are combinations of tones from the blues scales, "splanky" grace notes, and rolling triplet figures. They are great fun to play and give the music a forward motion and soulful sound.

Last, but not least, are the 16th-note right hand figures in bars 13-25 of the solo. They reflect Charlie Parker's bebop influence on Hampton. It is important to play these slowly at first and find fingerings that allow you to smoothly connect the notes. Once you have accomplished this, transpose your favorite passages into all keys and add them to your growing collection of improvisational ideas.

There is much more to discover in this transcription, and I hope you will continue to explore it on your own for examples of Hampton Hawes' style and characteristics of his truly unique voice among jazz pianists.

WHEN YOU WISH UPON A STAR

Arranged by ANDY LaVERNE

Words by NED WASHINGTON
Music by LEIGH HARLINE

When Francois LaCharme, the producer of my album *Natural Living*, suggested that I include "When You Wish Upon a Star," I responded enthusiastically. I've always considered this to be a very poignant and beautiful composition. I decided to treat the tune as delicately as possible.

The tune is originally in the key of C major, but I feel that it has a richer, darker quality in the key of E♭. The form is *AABA*. I harmonize the first two *A* sections rather sparsely, except measure 4, which has contrary motion between the melody and bass. The *B* section starts with a B♭ pedal point, which gives way to more active root movement. The final *A* section is a bit more active harmonically than the preceding sections. Bar 4 of the final *A* is an arpeggiated figure based on the harmonies of the fourth bar of the first two *A* sections. Bars 22-23 contain the most lush harmonies in the tune, with a different dominant chord and some alteration assigned to each melody note. The deceptive cadence in the last bar

finally resolves to E♭ major.

If you wish to improvise over these changes, I suggest that you use the left hand voicings given and an appropriate chord scale in the right hand for your note choices. Some possibilities are

m7 and **m6** chords - Dorian mode
dom7 and **7(sus)** chords - Mixolydian mode
dom7 with ♭9, +9, ♭13 (+5) - Superlocrian (altered) scale
dom7 with +11 - Lydian ♭7
dom7 with ♭9 - half/whole diminished scale
diminished chord - whole/half diminished scale
minor chord with **Ma7** - ascending melodic minor
Ma7 - Ionian or Lydian mode
Ma7 with +5 - Lydian augmented

• • •

One final comment: play this piece with a somewhat *rubato* feel, with a lot of expression, and perhaps your wish will come true!

— *Andy LaVerne*

We were talking about how to create chord symbols for this arrangement, and Clare Fischer quoted an accomplished West coast musician who had told him, "Don't ever write anything beyond the seventh. I never pay any attention to it anyway." Fischer went on to tell me that he doesn't even write with key signatures because his writing is so chromatic.

With Clare Fischer, voicings become as much a part of the song and the sound as the melody. In his harmonic scheme, almost very chord contains the resolution of a prior temnsion and the appearance of a new one. "When You Wish Upon A Star" unfolds in this fashion. Chord symbols don't seem appropriate.

Fischer began his career as a musical director for the vocal group the Hi-Lo'. His more recent groups have been vocal (2 + 2) and Latin (Salsa Picante). Fischer records on Discovery Records (P.O. Box 48081, Los Angeles , CA 90048) in many settings — big band, solo, Latin group, small ensamble, with Jerry Coker....Fischer writes for all.   – Becca Pulliam

WHEN YOU WISH UPON A STAR

Arranged by CLARE FISCHER

Music by LEIGH HARLINE

Chord voicings for solo piano
Noreen Sauls

"Slash Chords" are the chord symbols that use the following format: right hand chord/left hand root or chord

The abbreviation "Ped" on the left side signifies that a single note bass is wanted, not a left hand chord. By indicating what pitches belong in each hand, slash symbols sketch the chord voicing.

Noreen Sauls' ballad "What Might Have Been" begins with a slash chord. She also uses complex symbols with single note roots and chord extensions (9ths, 11ths, or 13ths) and alterations (sharped or flatted tones). In her article, she presents an approach to voicing these complex symbols. The approach will be just as helpful on other pieces as on her lovely ballad. — Ed.

To the inexperienced player and even to the more practiced one, some of these extended and altered chords may seem totally overwhelming. Or, if you spent years learning to sightread complex symbols, the occasional slash chord may leave you scratching your head. However, once you break down the song and the symbols in a logical manner, the situation won't look nearly so hopeless!

You're ready to tackle the symbols. They present information logically, from left to right. So first, note the root and the quality of the third (major or minor). Then, note the type of seventh (major or dominant). In solo piano, the root, seventh and third — and possibly the unaltered fifth — will usually go in the left hand. They create a harmonically firm foundation.

Now, begin looking at the extensions and alterations. The extensions are 9ths, 11ths, and 13ths. Don't let these higher numbers confuse you. Just keep in mind that the 9th is your 2nd scale tone, the 11th is your 4th, and the 13th is your 6th scale tone. Because they're an octave above the lower tones, they're called the extensions. Next, look for the alterations: sharped (+) or flatted 5ths, 9ths, 11ths, and 13ths. In solo piano, extensions and alterations are likely to be voiced by the right hand. Many times, they are the melody notes themselves.

Fine tuning your voicing

Once you have found all of the chord tones, then you must place each tone properly to obtain a good voicing.

In the arrangement of "What Might Have Been," the intervals in the left hand are mostly open sevenths and tenths. Since there are a lot of people who can't reach a tenth (including me), these will have to be rolled. This won't be too difficult because the 5th is placed between the root and the 10th. Look at measures 1 and 10 for examples. You can pedal the root lightly and easily

roll up to the 10th, using the 5th as an "anchor." Be sure to pedal cleanly, so the harmonies don't "bleed" into one another.

Besides sevenths and tenths, I've used thirds (bars 2, 3), fifths (bars 20, 25), and broken chords (bar 23) in the left hand. The seventh-leading-to-the-third progression*(bars 2, 3, and 15-16) has a particularly balanced feeling as the two voices move toward one another. I recommend turning this into a separate exercise by taking the left hand chords that appear in measures 15 and 16 and running them up the keyboard as shown in the figure below.

In general, I did not double*the chord tones in these voicings. There is usually no need to do so. In many cases doubling chord tones makes the voicings too ponderous. However, from just before measure 22 through measure 27, I have deliberately doubled the right hand melody in octaves, placing the other chord tones in between. I did this to give the melodic line more strength and to make the chords sound more balanced. Check the difference for yourself. First, play this section as written. Then play it again, leaving out the bottom note of the right hand so you can hear the difference in the sound.

Finally, throughout the piece there are places where I have included some very close intervals — major and minor seconds. At first these close intervals may sound strange and very dissonant; but, as you play them and really get the sound in your ear, they will begin to sound rich and wonderful.

Practice and experiment with all kinds of voicings and find the sounds that please your ear. Always remember the importance of playing in a variety of keys and transposing what you have learned from one key to another. When you learn a good voicing in one key, transpose it and learn it in others, and you'll multiply its potential uses. Learning to handle these complex chords is certainly a challenge, but the end result makes it all worthwhile! ●

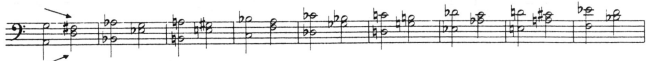

WHAT MIGHT HAVE BEEN

NOREEN SAULS
(1956-   )

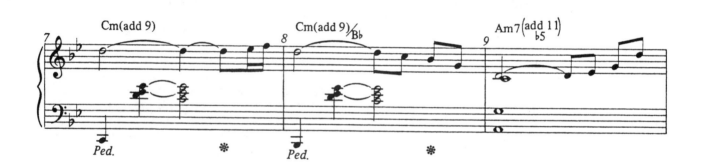

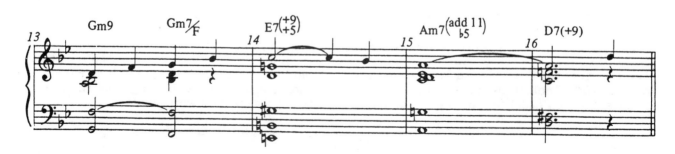

222

223

WRAP YOUR TROUBLES IN DREAMS

as played on Art Tatum: Piano Solo Private Sessions October 1952
New York Jazz Anthology 550052

Words by TED KOEHLER and BILLY MOLL
Music by HARRY BARRIS

Chord symbols are simplified.

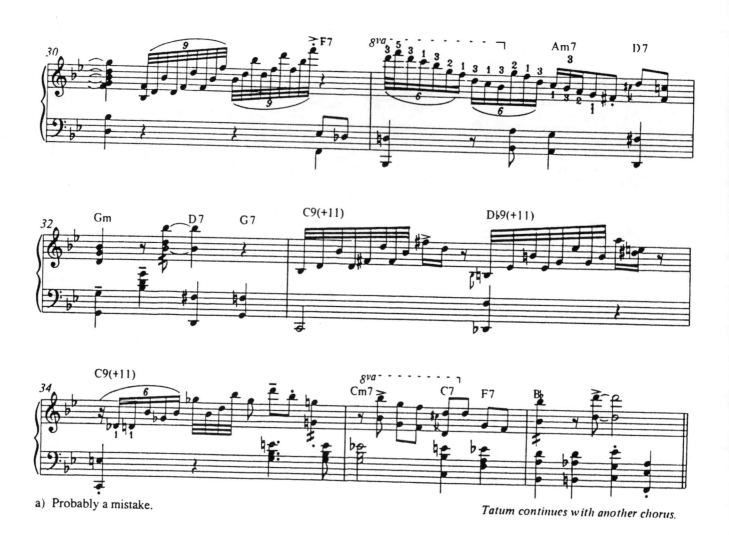

a) Probably a mistake.

Tatum continues with another chorus.

THE PEACOCKS

Written and arranged by JIMMY ROWLES
(1918-   )

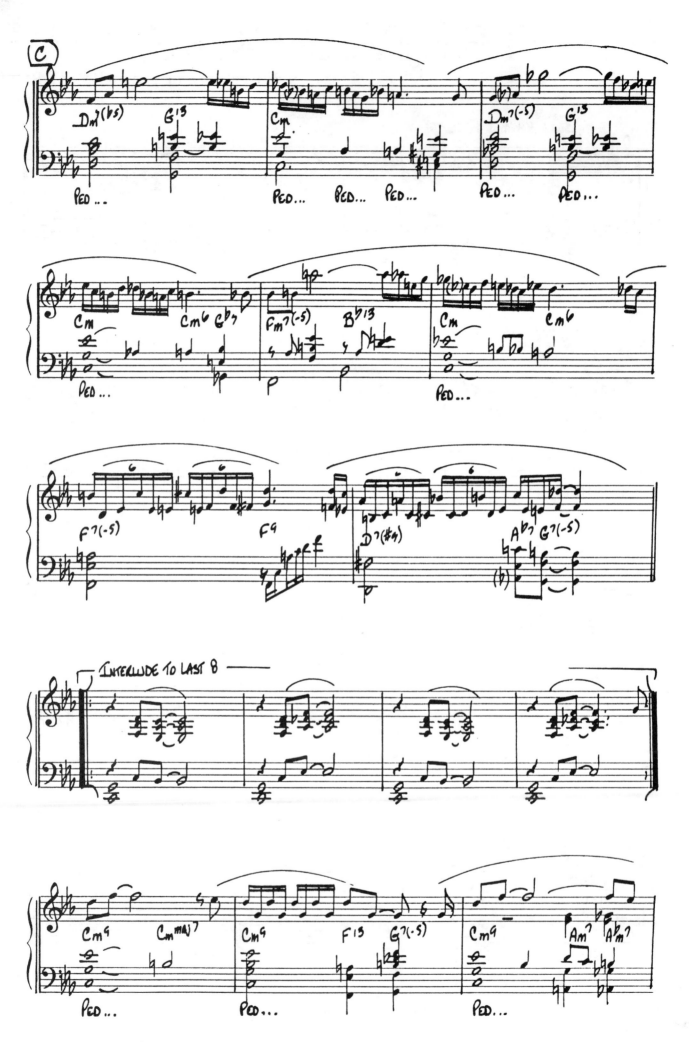

228